Little Freddie
at the Kentucky Derby

Little Freddie at the Kentucky Derby

KATHRYN COCQUYT

ILLUSTRATED BY
SYLVIA CORBETT

PELICAN PUBLISHING COMPANY
Gretna 1995

First printing, 1992
Second printing, 1995

Library of Congress Cataloging-in-Publication Data

Cocquyt, Kathryn.
    Little Freddie at the Kentucky Derby / Kathryn
Cocquyt ; illustrated by Sylvia Corbett.
       p. cm.
    Summary: Follows a young colt named Little Freddie from
his foal days on a racing farm until he wins the Kentucky
Derby.
    ISBN 0-88289-856-6. — ISBN 1-56554-159-6 (pbk.)
    1. Horses—Juvenile Fiction. [1. Horses—Fiction. 2. Horse
racing—Fiction.] I. Corbett, Sylvia, ill. II. Title.
PZ10.3.C645Li   1992
[Fic]—dc20   91-23540
                                           CIP
                                           AC

Jacket illustration by Chip Pace
Jacket design by Jason Allen

Manufactured in the United States of America
Published by Pelican Publishing Company, Inc.
1101 Monroe Street, Gretna, Louisiana 70053

To Peter Heindl and Romantic Myth,
for all the love they shared with us.

Contents

Little Freddie
at the Kentucky Derby

CHAPTER ONE

A Foal

HIS ARRIVAL WAS WATCHED over by a young stablehand. The boy smiled as the foal took his first breath of the crisp early morning air.

"It's a chestnut colt, Mama. He's a handsome one!" the boy said.

The little horse lay exhausted. The straw underneath him rustled with each shallow breath he took, as his mother gently nuzzled his frail body. He looked about with blurry, new-born eyes, viewing his surroundings with an innocence that only a baby horse could have. Instinctively, he knew that the mare looking over him so protectively was his mother.

He struggled to get to his feet. With his first attempt to stand on his long, wobbly legs he fell back to the ground. Romantic Myth put her nose under his front legs and propped him to his feet. He stood precariously, on his own for the first time. Hesitantly, he took a step, and then another. He stumbled as he turned to come back to her. The stablehand chuckled softly as the colt stood again, by himself, and wobbled to his mother.

"That's pretty good, little guy, considering you're only ten minutes old," he said.

The foal's coat was a beautiful deep chestnut color with no white markings at all. His eyes were kind like his mother's, and becoming more alert.

"His name will be Rue Royale, you know. But we can call him anything we want," the stablehand said to the mare.

Romantic Myth was proud of her new colt. "I'll call you Freddie," she said only loud enough for the foal to hear.

Freddie was the name of a groom Romantic Myth had known during her days at the racetrack. He had been at her side in her victories and defeats, and had remained her steadfast friend throughout. Although many years had passed since she had seen him, she always remembered his kindness. The gentle look of her new foal reminded her of her old friend.

"He would be proud to know I named you after him."

The stablehand patted the mare softly and left them to the stillness of the night.

And so it was that a chestnut colt came into the world on the last day of April, just hours before dawn.

He opened his eyes to the sun rising over a hill at the east end of the pasture. Sunlight filled the sky, making the paths along the hillside golden ribbons that disappeared into the treeline at its crest. The rest of the mares and the foals in the herd were still huddled together for warmth.

As he focused his sleepy eyes he saw a nest of baby birds in the tree above. Their chirps were loud and frantic as their tiny beaks reached for the food their mother offered. It was morning, little Freddie's favorite time of day. He sprang to his feet so fast that he almost lost his balance. Only days old, he was still wrestling with the forces of gravity.

There were many things he wanted to do, and they all raced through his mind in an instant. What could he do first? Maybe he would stand by the feeder so he and his mother would be the first ones to the grain when the farm help came to feed them. Or maybe he would jump in the air and make the other foals wake up and run with him.

Little Freddie was a very mischievous colt. His mother was considered too lenient by the other mares in the pasture. They thought she let him have too much freedom and not enough discipline.

"Your colt is always getting into trouble!" said Silverblue.

Silverblue liked to remind Freddie's mother that between them, she had won more prize money on the racetrack. Silverblue had had a long and hard career as a racehorse. An injury had made her right leg crooked and swollen, and now she was unable to run at all. Even walking a short distance was hard for her. She had nothing much to do these days except talk at length about her days at the track.

"I know," Romantic Myth admitted. "He doesn't mean to be any trouble, he's just spirited."

"Well," huffed Silverblue. "My foals have all won very important races. I have been very strict with each of them. None of your foals have ever won a race because you never gave them proper discipline. You let them do whatever they want—Freddie is a perfect example of that."

Romantic Myth said nothing. She gave a little smile to Silverblue's colt, Thunderball, who stood obediently at his mother's side. She understood that the mare's lameness had made her bitter and old before her time. She remembered what a beautiful horse she used to be when they raced against each other. Her tall, sleek stature made her faster than Romantic Myth, but she was not liked very much by the other horses. Silverblue was always too proud to give them a kind word, even when they won.

Just then little Freddie ran up to them like a gust of wind.

"Come on, Mother, let's run!" he said as he came to a halt in front of them, with dust rising up in their faces.

Thunderball cocked his head to one side and looked at little Freddie. "Why are you so excited all the time?" Thunderball asked.

"I dunno," Freddie answered, cocking his head the same way as Thunderball. Then in an instant he was gone, running full speed toward the middle of the pasture.

Thunderball was little Freddie's best friend. He liked the way Freddie was so happy all the time, and how he was never scared, even when the wind blew across the pasture and lightning flashed in the sky. Freddie would always comfort him by telling him that nothing bad would happen to them, although the roaring thunder sometimes made Thunderball wonder.

He would have liked to run and play more, but his mother told him that true champion racehorses were dignified, in control of themselves at all times. She would have preferred that Thunderball choose another colt as his best friend, one who was not as rambunctious and who came from a winning bloodline. Thunderball knew how she felt, but Freddie always looked like he was having so much fun.

"They're coming, they're coming," Freddie called to Thunderball. "They're coming with the hay. Come here, Thunderball, I can see them loading it into the truck."

Thunderball looked at Silverblue, silently asking her permission to join Freddie at the far end of the pasture.

Silverblue frowned. "Don't get into the habit of waiting like that little beggar Freddie."

"He's always the first one to the grain," Thunderball protested.

Silverblue's brows knitted together, her look stern. "There would be enough grain for everyone if Freddie did not try to take it all. No discipline or manners, and all spirit. He'll be a handful to train—he's a handful now."

Thunderball bowed his head.

The sound of the truck grew louder and it was soon in sight. Little Freddie became more excited the closer it came. He ran back toward his mother and the others.

"You see," he said, "I knew they were coming. I could see them way over by the barn."

Silverblue glared back at him. "You are a colt with good eyesight and bad manners," she said gruffly and hobbled away.

Thunderball followed, looking back at little Freddie as if he did not want to go. "I'll see you later, OK Freddie?"

"OK, Thunderball, I'll see you later," he answered, wondering why Silverblue never had anything nice to say to him.

"Silverblue doesn't like me very much, does she, Mother?" he asked Romantic Myth.

"No Freddie, I don't think so," she answered.

"But why not? I like her a lot, and Thunderball is my best friend."

"I think she would like you to be more in control of yourself. You have so much spirit she worries that you are a bad example for Thunderball. He would like to do the things that you do, and she thinks he shouldn't."

"But that's just the way I am. I can't be any other way," he said, concerned.

Romantic Myth nodded. "I know. Being yourself is fine with me. You can't be something you're not, no matter what others may want," she replied. "Now don't spend so much time worrying about it or you'll miss breakfast."

Freddie looked up to see that the rest of the herd had already started eating and hurried over to the feeder to get his morning ration of hay.

CHAPTER TWO

A Spring Day

SPRING IS A TIME of rebirth. The once barren trees blossom into bright green leafy umbrellas. Tiny yellow florets bloom on the undergrowth and bring the rabbits out of the thickets to feast after enduring the cold winter.

It is the time when nature celebrates itself with gentle rainshowers and the sweet aroma of fresh anise and wildflowers. It is a time when baby horses are born to serenade the lush pastures with the sound of tiny hooves running behind their mothers along the fence rails. With balletlike grace they display the dignity inherited through their breed. As the sun warms them during midday naps, the wind carries the newness of their surroundings to flared nostrils.

Little Freddie loved being with his mother and playing with his friends. Each day he learned something new, and with each setting sun his world was defined more and more by the white, four-board fence that marked the grassy pasture.

One afternoon when he was grazing underneath the shade

of an oak tree, he heard a strange sound from above. He pricked an ear to listen, thinking that maybe it was a new bird nesting, but the sound was very different from any of the birds he had heard before.

"Meow."

Freddie looked up.

"Meow."

He heard the sound again and looked up into the tree to see a kitten sitting on the highest branch of the giant oak.

"Meow!" the kitten cried, and little Freddie could see by the look in her eyes that she was very frightened.

"Hello," Freddie said, trying to be friendly.

"Meow," the kitten cried again. "Can you get me down?"

"Who me?" Freddie asked. "I can't climb a tree, I'm a colt! How did you get up there?"

The bewildered kitten looked down at him. "I was running from the coyote that lives in the thicket on the hill. He was going to get me, and this was the only place I could go to get away."

Freddie's eyes widened with surprise. "He was going to get you?" He paused, "What's your name?"

"My name is Patches. My mother named me that because my coat has orange and black circles. She says it looks like patches on a white coat."

Freddie smiled. Patches was the first animal he had met that wasn't a horse. "My name is Freddie, and my mother is Romantic Myth. Where's your mother?"

The little kitten suddenly became sad and tears filled her eyes. "She was hit by a car when we crossed the highway last night. She's dead."

Little Freddie felt very sorry for the kitten. He could not imagine how lonely he would be if his mother died and left him alone. He wanted to do something to make her happy again.

"I'm sorry about your mother, but maybe you could live here. Even though you're not a horse you might not mind it too much. I wouldn't let the coyote chase you. I would kick him, like that." Little Freddie kicked his hind legs in the air showing what he would do to the coyote. "After all, where else can you go without a mother?"

The forlorn kitten looked back at him with sad eyes. She had been so busy trying to survive the night that she had not fully realized how alone she was until now.

"I don't know what I should do," she said, rubbing her tired eyes with her paws.

"Do you have any brothers or sisters?"

Patches perked up. "I have two brothers. One is all orange like this spot," she pointed to the orange spot on her side. "The other one is all black, like this spot, except for one white paw." She pointed to the spot on her other side.

Freddie laughed and Patches laughed with him.

"Where are they?" Freddie asked.

"The coyote chased them too. We all ran as fast as we could, and I ran up this tree. He wasn't going to get me, I'm the fastest climber there is," she said proudly. "My brothers must be nearby, but I haven't seen them all day."

"I'm sure you will all get back together soon."

"Yes, I'm sure. I know how to hunt for food, my mother showed me. There's plenty of water, too, so I guess I'll be all right. I just wish I wasn't alone. I've never been alone before."

Freddie was sympathetic. He had never been alone either. His mother was his teacher and protector. There was nothing better than taking a walk with her around the pasture as she told stories about her racing days. She would graze between sentences, and Freddie would wait anxiously for her to continue with her story. He never tried to hurry her though, because when she finished the story that meant their walk was through, and he never wanted it to end.

"Would you like to live here with me and my mother?" he asked again, hoping to make Patches feel better.

Just then a sound came from the ground under Freddie's nose. He looked down to see a tiny pink dot poking out from a hole in the ground. It was a nose with little whiskers bristling on either side. As it poked its head out further Freddie could see two very large ears. It was a mouse, and he climbed out and looked up in the tree to the branch where Patches was sitting.

"Well, you can't stay here!" the mouse declared. "I live here under this oak tree. I've lived here for years and I'm not about to move because some orphaned cat decides she doesn't want to be alone. You hear me?"

Both Freddie and Patches looked back at the mouse in surprise. They could not believe that something so small could be so unafraid.

"Do you hear me?" the mouse turned and pointed at Freddie.

"But—but, Patches has no place to go. Her mother was killed last night, and her brothers are lost."

The mouse shook his head emphatically. "That's no problem of mine. My only concern is for me, and I know for a fact that my life will be very short indeed if some cat moves into this neighborhood. They eat mice you know, hunt them down and kill them. So you just move along and take your cat friend with you."

Freddie looked up at Patches. "He thinks if you live here that you'll eat him. Would you do that?"

Patches shook her head.

"She says she wouldn't do that," Freddie explained to the mouse.

The mouse folded his arms across his chest and curled his long tail around one foot. "I don't believe her. I've never met a cat that got along with a mouse. Every cat I've ever known has killed mice, eaten them too. Why, with the way they hunt us down, it's a wonder there's a mouse left in the world."

"Oh, I wouldn't do something like that," Patches protested sincerely. "I wouldn't want to kill you, Mr. Mouse. Why, I would like to be your friend. I could be the first cat to be friends with a mouse."

"Absolutely not," the mouse stated. "There is not a cat on earth that could be friends with a mouse. Besides, none of my friends would associate with me anymore. I'd be an outcast."

Discouraged, Patches sank back onto the branch trying to think of some way to convince the mouse she was telling the truth. She needed a friend now more than anything. Freddie felt the same, and tried again to change the mouse's mind.

"Well, the only reason a cat kills mice is for food. If the owners of this farm take Patches in, she will have plenty of food, and there would be no reason for her to bother you, right?" Freddie offered.

The mouse thought for a moment. He put his paw to his

chin and scratched, looking pensively at the kitten, then at Freddie.

"I suppose," he said finally.

Patches' ears perked up and a smile came to her face. "Then, if I could get these people to feed me, would you still mind if I stayed?"

"No, I guess not. But they would have to want to feed you, that's the only way."

Freddie was relieved. "Good, now Patches, you just have to go to the house and meow. They're really nice and I'm sure they'll want to keep you."

Patches nodded. "OK, I'll try."

Carefully she found her way down the oak tree. She looked at Freddie hesitantly. "Do you think they'll like me?"

"Oh sure. Just look confident," Freddie replied.

The kitten headed for the side door with her tail sticking straight up in the air and a spring to her step. Halfway there she jumped up and tried to catch a butterfly that flew by. Freddie glanced at the mouse.

"Cats are trouble," the mouse sneered.

Freddie said nothing. He did not want to encourage any dislike the mouse already had for Patches.

The kitten made it to the side porch and sat with her head tilted to one side, meowing sweetly. In a few moments the door opened and out came the lady who lived there.

"You're just a baby," she said cuddling Patches. "You need some warm milk."

She kissed the kitten on the forehead and took her inside.

"There, you see?" Freddie said to the mouse. "Now she can stay just like you said."

The mouse frowned and began shaking his finger at Freddie. "Yes, she can stay. But I'm holding you responsible, young man, if anything goes wrong! You hear me?"

Freddie nodded.

"A cat being friends with a mouse! I've never heard of such a thing," he mumbled to himself as he went into his hole.

Freddie watched the mouse until he was out of sight. He wondered why the mouse could not be as happy as he was that Patches would be living there.

"Hey Freddie, come here," someone called from the other end of the pasture.

It was Revolver, a bay colt. He was bigger than the other colts and he used his strength to bully them.

"What?" Freddie called back.

"Come over here, we're having races and I've beaten all the rest of these guys. Now I want to beat you!" Revolver challenged.

Freddie knew that Revolver was bigger than he was, but he had watched him run and did not think Revolver was very agile because of his size. Still, Freddie had never raced against him and thought it might be fun.

"OK," Freddie agreed and went to where Revolver and the other colts were standing.

Six colts had gathered around Revolver. Each had taken his turn racing against him and each had lost—except Thunderball, who had tied. Of course, Revolver refused to admit that Thunderball was equally as fast as he was, and rather than argue with him Thunderball thought it would be better if he could help Freddie beat him altogether.

"Freddie," Thunderball whispered. "I've got to tell you something."

"Yes?"

"I almost beat him, but he cut in front of me at the last minute on the turn just before you get to the gate. He'll wait until you're out of sight from the rest of us, then he'll cross your path just enough to break your stride. Don't run as fast as you can before he does that. Run just enough to stay with him, then after he cuts you off give it all you've got and you'll beat him," Thunderball advised.

"OK, enough talking," Revolver interrupted. "Are you going to race or not?"

"Sure," Freddie answered. "Where do you want to start?"

"We start at this fence and go up the hill to the gate at the far end. You got that?"

Freddie nodded.

"Thunderball, you say go," Revolver commanded.

Thunderball waited longer than usual to start the race. He wanted to let Freddie have enough time to choose his path and be on a good starting foot so that he would have every chance to win. He did not like the way Revolver tried to intimidate the other colts in the pasture, and most of all he did not like the way he wanted to win even if it meant cheating.

"On your mark, get set, go!" he yelled, and Freddie and Revolver took off with divots of grass shooting up behind them as they ran.

They all watched as Freddie paced himself and held back as much as he could, waiting for Revolver to make his move. They went up the hill and for just a moment disappeared behind its incline. When they reappeared Freddie was clearly in the lead, running at full stride to the gate to finish first.

The other colts cheered for Freddie. Since they had all lost to Revolver, Freddie's victory was all the more impressive. They had not heard Thunderball's advice, and he thought it all the better that it remain a secret between the two of them. He was glad that Revolver had been put in his place by his best friend. If Revolver had won instead of Freddie, there would have been no end to his boasting.

The two colts walked back to the herd. Freddie was tired, but happy to have won the contest. His head was high and there was a spring to his gait that made him look more proud of himself than he would have liked to let on.

Revolver was stunned by his defeat. He thought that he could not have possibly lost to a younger colt like Freddie.

"He cheated!" Revolver declared.

Freddie could not believe that Revolver would be such a poor loser.

"No I didn't. I won that race fair and square."

"He's right," Thunderball agreed. "It's just a race for fun. Freddie wouldn't cheat—you are the one who cheated."

Revolver glared at Thunderball. "Are you calling me a liar?"

"You cut me off when we raced."

Everyone was silent. Revolver knew that Thunderball had seen him cheating, but now everyone else believed it, too.

"I won't forget this," he glared at Thunderball. "Next time I'll really beat you, then you'll be sorry."

Thunderball and Freddie did not bother to respond to his threat as they turned and walked away.

Later that day Freddie was thinking about the race and wanted to thank Thunderball for his advice. He found him standing under the oak tree, watching the mockingbird busily at work building a new nest.

"What are you looking at?" Freddie asked.

"That mockingbird is making a new nest for her children. The wind blew so hard last night that it scattered the twigs and knocked the old one down. I guess they were getting too big for it anyway."

Freddie looked up and saw the bird weaving a piece of cotton in amongst the branches.

"Do you think she minds having to change homes?"

Thunderball shook his head. "No, I think she knows that it's time to make a new one. Someday we could have another home, too."

Freddie thought a moment. "I would rather stay here."

"Me, too," Thunderball agreed. "Boy, I'm sure glad you beat Revolver today. Did he try to cut you off like I said?"

"Yep, he sure did, but I remembered what you told me and I was waiting for it. Thanks a lot."

Thunderball smiled. "Sure. Revolver wants to win so much that he'll cheat to do it. I'm glad you spoiled his plans."

Freddie shook his head. He was glad that he had such a good friend in Thunderball. He watched the bird carry a piece of string to one side of the nest, tuck it under a branch, then carry it to the other side. He supposed he would not mind having a new home if he could still be with his mother. He thought of Patches. She had to make a new home alone, but she did not seem to mind. She was just happy to be in a place where they liked her and gave her fresh milk to drink.

The sun was setting over the hilltop, and the mockingbird was quickly becoming a silhouette in the evening sky. It had been a busy day.

The next afternoon as Romantic Myth stood over Freddie while he napped, a big truck with a horse trailer pulled up to the pasture gate. Romantic Myth recognized the horse trailer. She had ridden in it many times before.

She watched the driver go into the farm office and come back out with two stablehands. One of them pointed at her as they entered the pasture.

"Freddie," she nuzzled him gently to wake him. "Get up now."

Freddie opened his sleepy eyes. "Why mother?"

"Because we are going somewhere today. Somewhere new."

When Freddie saw the men coming toward him he jumped to his feet. Startled, he stood behind his mother for protection.

One of the men hooked a lead rope to Romantic Myth's halter and started walking to the truck. Freddie followed, keeping a close eye on the other two men. He did not know them, and like most colts his age he was not used to being touched by people. All he knew was that they were taking them away from the pasture he had always known as home, and he did not like it.

They stopped in front of the trailer and led Romantic Myth inside. Freddie was too frightened to follow. It was a dark, narrow place, and had only one door. Since the day he was born he had always been outside. All of his natural instincts told him not to go into this strange-looking thing.

"Freddie, come in here," his mother said.

Freddie shook his head. "No, you come out here. I think we should go back with Silverblue and Thunderball."

Suddenly, one of the men grabbed him at the withers, the other at his hindquarters, and they lifted him into the trailer. The door slammed shut with a thunderous roar before he knew what had happened. He stood paralyzed in the middle of the trailer. The loud engine echoed through the small room as the ground began to move under his feet. It was strange to see the floor perfectly still while the trees on either side of him whizzed by.

He stumbled to catch his balance as they rounded the curve of the driveway and turned onto the main road. He looked back to see Thunderball and Silverblue at the far end of the pasture. They stood next to the fence. Patches was perched in a nearby tree watching the trailer drive away. In that moment Freddie realized that he was being taken away from his home without even having a chance to say goodbye to his friends.

For a long time he was silent. The heat of the midday sun and the sounds of passing cars compounded the abrupt flashes of blurry scenery. He was sad and nervous. He had been taken from his friends and the place he cared most about.

"Where are we going?" he asked Romantic Myth.

She looked at her foal with such a sympathetic expression that Freddie found it hard to be upset.

"We're going to our owners' home," she answered.

"Our owners' home? But they come to visit us at the farm. Why do we have to leave?"

Over the last three months he had come to know everyone in the pasture. Romantic Myth could scarcely remember how she had felt when she had to leave friends and places behind for the first time. She knew that this was the first of many new places Freddie would see in his lifetime as a racehorse. There would be different stables and racetracks where he would stay, sometimes only for a day. When he raced there would be the places he knew as home, and finally when his racing days were over there would be a place where he would retire. Yet, for now, explaining why he had to leave his friends was a difficult task for her.

"Freddie," she said softly. "I know that it is hard for you to understand why we have to leave the pasture. All I can tell you is what I've learned from my own experiences. Every time I was taken to a different place it was for a reason. There will be many new places in your life. You may be very happy in some of them and not so happy in others, but changes are a part of life."

Freddie's eyes looked sad and empty. She knew how he missed the pasture already. Still, she could not know if they would ever return to the place where he was born or see Thunderball and Patches again.

"But what about Thunderball? He's my best friend. He'll miss me if I don't come back," Freddie protested.

"Yes, I'm sure he will. The same way you'll miss him. But soon you'll make new friends and even though you still think of him, it won't be as hard."

Freddie shook his head. "I'll never forget about him. You haven't forgotten about your friends. All those stories you told me when we would take walks together, they were all about your friends and the things you did together."

Romantic Myth comforted her colt. "Yes they were, but I am not with them now, and they are still my friends.

"True friends don't stop caring for you just because you're far away. Sometimes you may never see them again, but you think of them and remember them for the rest of your life, and their love is always in your heart."

She knew by his softened eyes and lowered ears that her words had calmed him.

"You mean that someday I could see Thunderball again and he'll still be my best friend?"

"Yes," she answered.

"And if I don't see him for the rest of my life, he'll still be my friend, too?"

Romantic Myth nodded and nuzzled him affectionately.

The trailer turned into a small side street. Freddie stretched high to look out the window. There was a house with a pasture next to it. Although it was much smaller than the one where he was born, it still had plenty of room to run.

At the very end of the pasture, closest to the road, stood two horses. One was brown with a white star on her forehead, the other was grey. They both followed the trailer curiously as it pulled down the road and stopped at the gate. The brown horse was the first to look inside.

Recognizing Romantic Myth, she let out a squeal of delight. Romantic Myth answered excitedly.

"Mother, do you know her?" Freddie asked.

"Yes, her name is Mardi Gras. She is one of those friends I was telling you about."

CHAPTER THREE

Freddie's New Home

LITTLE FREDDIE LIKED THIS new place. It overlooked a river, and was surrounded by hillsides covered with oak trees. There were three eucalyptus trees at the end of the pasture, and each afternoon when the breeze blew up the river valley from the sea he could smell their mild aroma.

He was brought to the pasture each day for exercise and he would run as fast as he could while his mother looked on. Freddie could not help but think of Thunderball during these times and wonder how he was. He wondered how long he would be here before he would meet someone his own age, someone who liked to play the way Thunderball did.

Freddie liked his owners very much. They were a man and a woman. The woman had a funny laugh and brown specks across her nose. Romantic Myth explained to him that humans called these specks freckles. The man was taller than she was, with a calm voice and a gentle manner.

Sometimes in the afternoons the woman would bring Freddie a carrot to eat, or offer all of the horses some extra alfalfa hay, and talk kindly to them before going back into the house. The man liked to scratch Freddie between his ears and down the front of his chest, because he knew Freddie liked the way it felt.

Each evening when the sun was fading from the sky and all of the horses were happily eating their hay, both the man and woman would visit with them. They always gave them plenty to eat. Though he was still nursing, Freddie quickly became accustomed to eating hay and grain. It made him feel just like the older horses. He even had his own bucket.

Romantic Myth and Freddie had their own stall, too. It was made of four wooden boards on all sides and painted white, just like the rest of the ranch fence. The gate that opened out into the pasture had spaces big enough for Freddie to put his head through so that he could munch on the grass growing around the outer fenceposts.

One day he saw his owners coming up the drive toward his stall, only this time they had someone else with them. It was a girl with hair the color of straw. Freddie recognized her from when he was at the farm. She had tried to catch him once when she had visited.

There were two dogs that ran alongside them. One had a shiny black coat that shone almost blue in the sunlight and the other was a golden shepherd. They jumped and tumbled to the ground as they wrestled happily with each other. They seemed unusually glad to see each other, and watching them play made Freddie miss Thunderball even more.

As they approached, Freddie could see that he had caught the eye of the shepherd. He came toward Freddie, leaving the black dog wondering where he was. He ran underneath the fence and into the stall. Startled by his forwardness, Freddie cautiously stepped back. His mother stayed by the wall and paid little attention to them.

The dog looked at Freddie as if he were trying to figure out just what he was. In a moment the black dog joined him but stayed a good distance away, hiding behind the shepherd.

"Are you a horse?" the shepherd asked.

Freddie's ears perked up at the question. "Who me?" he asked.

"Yeah, you. Are you a little horse or a big dog?" he asked again.

The black dog stepped out from behind the shepherd to get a closer look. "I think he's a big dog," she offered, straining her neck towards him with her nose quivering, trying to catch a scent.

Freddie took a step forward thinking she was trying to be friendly. When he was almost next to her she jumped back suddenly, startling them both.

"What are you so afraid of?" the shepherd asked her. "It doesn't look like he's gonna hurt anyone. Are you?"

"Me? No, I wouldn't hurt anyone," Freddie answered nervously.

The black dog was not convinced. The closer Freddie got the more she backed away.

"I don't know," she cautioned, "I've never seen a dog that big before, or a horse that small. What do you think he is?"

The shepherd shrugged. "I don't know. What are you, a dog or a horse?"

"I'm a colt," Freddie answered proudly, standing up very straight. "I'm a baby horse, and you two are dogs, aren't you?"

"Sure are. My name is Timber, this is Tane," the shepherd said motioning to the black dog. "She lives here. I'm just visiting for the weekend. How long are you going to be here?"

Freddie thought a moment. "I don't know. I have only been here a few days. I came from a farm, I think it's north of here, that's what I heard them say. I have a friend there, his name is Thunderball. We played together the way you and Tane were playing."

Timber smiled. He was the older, more experienced of the two dogs.

"How old are you?" Timber asked.

"I'm three months old. I'm little now, but someday I'm gonna be a racehorse," he answered confidently.

"Really? Hmm, I've never met a racehorse before," Timber replied.

"Timber, get out of the stall!" the girl with yellow hair yelled from the drive.

Timber sighed heavily. "Well, I got to go. I'll probably see you later," he said, then ran to her side with Tane right behind him.

Freddie watched suspiciously as his owners and the girl entered the stall. It was not a very big area and it made him nervous to have the three of them there. He went to his mother's side. She didn't seem too upset, and that reassured him.

The yellow-haired girl stood very still. Then she tried to touch him and he jumped in the air to get away. The man tried to stop him, but Freddie bucked and ran to the other side of the stall. His heart was pounding and he looked to his mother for reassurance. She still did not seem to mind.

He thought that maybe if he stayed very quiet and close to his mother they would soon leave him alone. Instead, they came to him again. This time they had him cornered, one on either side. With all his strength he bolted away. Each of them held him as long as they could, and Freddie carried them across the stall as he ran. Although he was only a few months old he was already quite strong—even stronger when frightened.

He went to the very corner of the stall and hid behind his mother. "She has to protect me," he thought to himself.

They approached him again, only this time he was unable to run. The man patted him softly on the neck; the blonde girl touched him on the back and spoke to him quietly. Freddie was scared for a moment until he realized that they were not trying to hurt him at all.

He relaxed and watched as the woman with the freckles came toward him with a halter. She touched him lightly on the nose, and gently put the halter over his face and around his neck, then buckled it on the side. Freddie could feel the slight pressure of the nose band, but her movements were deliberate and unthreatening.

When the halter was secured the people left. They wanted to give him time to get used to this new thing on his head.

"Mother, why did you let them put this on me?" he asked.

Romantic Myth tilted her head to look at him. He was still young and headstrong, but she wanted to impress upon him that when he was haltered he must be obedient. If he learned this lesson now from his owners he wouldn't have to learn it later from strangers at the racetrack who may not be as patient.

"A racehorse must learn to trust and obey his trainer. You must understand what is expected of you," she said. "The discipline that Silverblue talked about is important."

Freddie's eyes widened. "But Mother, I can run fast the way I am. Why should I let them tell me what to do?"

"You can be obedient and spirited. For a racehorse to be truly great he must understand what his rider expects of him. When you can work with others you can go on to achieve many things."

Little Freddie was quiet for a moment. This seemed so complicated. He didn't know how to tell which people were kind and which people were not. Everyone had been kind to him today, but he still did not like taking orders. He would rather not bother with manners at all and just run free in the pasture. Yet, he knew what his mother was saying was for the best. She would not have told it to him if it were not true.

He wiggled his nose, testing the strange feel of the leather halter.

"Yes, Mother," he frowned. "But this thing itches."

"You'll get used to it," she replied with a chuckle.

He wiggled his nose again, then went to the fence rail and rubbed his face against the wood to scratch.

It had been an eventful morning, and little Freddie could feel his lids growing heavy. He lay down and let the afternoon sun lull him to sleep.

CHAPTER FOUR

Freddie Learns
a Lesson

HALTER TRAINING HAD BEGUN. This meant that each day after Freddie's exercise, a lead rope was attached to his halter and he was led at his owner's side. He tried very hard to learn each command he was taught.

The owners would walk around the yard, stopping every so often so that Freddie could practice standing with his head upright. It showed that he had confidence in himself. Someday he would parade in the paddock before a race, and he was preparing now to look his best.

Before the daily lessons, his owner would always put Grant, the grey gelding, in a stall away from the other horses. Sometimes Mardi Gras, the brown mare, would walk with them, and other times she would watch from a distance. She never said much to little Freddie, but he sensed that she liked him. She was a good friend to his mother, and he could tell by the expression in her eyes that she was very sincere.

Freddie was not as sure about Grant, because he was very aggressive and liked to be the dominant horse in the pasture.

At times, little Freddie sensed that he did not like having a new colt there.

Wild horses share a fierce rivalry for leadership of a herd, sometimes fighting for superiority. Even though Freddie and Grant were not wild, there was an instinctive competition between them.

At feeding time, Romantic Myth and Freddie were put in their own stall while Grant and Mardi Gras were fed in the pasture. They would get into a spat almost every day, with Mardi Gras usually winning the argument. She would pin her ears back as a warning for Grant not to come any closer to her food. If he did, she would kick him with her back legs. He had marks on his hindquarters from the times she had set him straight about whose food belonged to whom.

Freddie always watched these fights with amusement, silently cheering Mardi Gras on. Yet, in spite of these quarrels, and the times he was schooled on his manners, Freddie's days were happily uneventful. He knew the daily routine and was very comfortable with it.

One day a car came down the drive and took Freddie by surprise. Startled, he got tangled in the stall gate, and fell to the other side. He was in the pasture with Grant, separated from his mother, and immediately realized that he was in danger. Unable to reach him either, Romantic Myth panicked. With her nose and front hoof she tried to push the gate open.

"Mother! I want to get back into the stall!" little Freddie cried.

"Just be calm, Freddie. I will get the gate open somehow."

Romantic Myth hurriedly pushed the gate harder, hoping to get through.

Suddenly, Freddie heard a whinny, and felt the ground underneath him rumble. From the corner of his eye he saw Grant charging at him as if he were his mortal enemy. Eyes glittering and teeth bared, Grant snapped his jaws shut as he tried to bite the colt. Freddie leaped out of his way but could feel his hot breath on his neck.

Grant composed himself in an instant. He snorted loudly and pawed the ground as he looked at Freddie with cold, steely eyes. Freddie had never been so close to the older gelding, and he looked like a giant to the little colt.

Fear rushed through his body so fast that he was hardly able to catch his breath. He did not know which way to turn. He tried to bolt to the stall gate, but Grant was there to block the way. Freddie cut quickly in the opposite direction to avoid him, but the gelding followed, cornering him near the outside fence.

Trapped, Freddie could only watch helplessly as Grant charged again. In the background he could faintly hear his mother calling. She was straining toward the fence, trying in vain to protect her colt.

The next few moments seemed like an eternity. Unable to look away from the savage stare of the oncoming horse, he knew there was no escaping the assault. He wished he were bigger, big enough to fight back, but it was only his quickness and agility that had saved him so far. If Grant came from one direction, Freddie could try to run the opposite way in time to avoid him. He only had to put his fear aside and wait for the right moment.

Grant was almost upon him, and Freddie was ready to make his move. In a moment Grant lunged forward, but to Freddie's surprise he was unable to reach him. Just then Mardi Gras charged in his path. Her ears were back and her teeth were showing, as she used her body to shield the young colt.

Stunned, Grant reared up on two legs, but Mardi Gras stood her ground. Freddie could see by the look in her eyes that she had changed from the normally kind horse she was to a wild-eyed protector, determined to do what she must to save him.

"Walk by my side until we reach your mother," she commanded, keeping her sights on Grant, who was following closely, still hoping for a chance to get at Freddie.

As they walked toward the stall he saw their owners rush out of the house, startled by the commotion. Freddie could not have been happier to see them now. Quickly, one of them ran to open the stall gate to reunite him with his mother.

Realizing that Freddie was beyond his reach, Grant became even more infuriated. He turned to Romantic Myth and tried to bite her on the neck, but she threw her head around, hitting him in the muzzle. She was more enraged than Mardi Gras. The gelding tried again to stop Mardi Gras from helping Freddie, but she turned and delivered a thunderous kick squarely to his chest.

Grant gasped with excruciating pain and backed away. Slowly his expression changed from anger to defeat. Mardi Gras and Romantic Myth remained steadfast, and he knew that they would only come back stronger if he persisted. He turned away and, hanging his head, walked into his open stall. The gate was shut behind him; the grey horse was no longer a threat to Freddie.

The quarrel was over. Romantic Myth and Mardi Gras relaxed. Even though they were very close friends, Romantic Myth felt indebted to Mardi Gras for her help.

"Thank you for protecting Freddie, Mardi Gras," she said sincerely.

The gentle expression returned to Mardi Gras's eyes. "That's all right. Grant shouldn't have been so rough with him. Freddie is too young to fight him alone."

She was too humble to take credit for saving Freddie from a fight that would have seriously hurt him, perhaps even killed him, because she had lived most of her life on the open range. She was a cattle horse and had to be very strong to endure the long hours of work in harsh conditions. What was considered something very extraordinary to other horses was part of daily life to a cattle horse. It was understood that each horse looked out for the other, and they never expected any special recognition for helping in a time of need.

"I know," Romantic Myth replied. "Still, if you hadn't been there to help I wouldn't want to think of what might have happened. You're a very good friend."

"Thank you," Mardi Gras said, bowing her head. "I know you would have done the same for me."

"Yes, I would have. I hope that someday I can return the favor. Freddie will always remember this too, won't you Freddie?" his mother said, nudging him.

"Huh?" Freddie asked. His gaze fixed on Grant, he had not been paying attention to their conversation.

"You won't forget what Mardi Gras did, will you?" she

asked again, in a tone of voice that made him realize that she was waiting for him to thank Mardi Gras as well.

"Uh-uh, I won't forget it. Boy, I sure am glad you were there to help out, but I think I could have handled him alone," the colt said bravely. "You know what? One of these days when I'm bigger I think I might just come back here and let him have it. Just like you did, just like that."

Mardi Gras looked him squarely in the eye. "Someday you might have to protect yourself, and I hope that because of this you'll understand how important it is to be fair. When you are the stronger one perhaps you'll be able to fight anyone and win, but it is better to use that strength to help those in need. Never fight just to show how tough you can be," she said.

Little Freddie was surprised to hear Mardi Gras say this. She had rarely spoken to him since the day he arrived. She glanced at Grant, who by now had seemingly forgotten everything and was munching on some hay.

"Grant only did what his instincts told him to do," she continued. "He knows that you are not his colt, and that someday you might challenge him. He wanted you to know that he was the strongest horse here, that's all. You might have to do the same someday, and decide for yourself what is fair."

Mardi Gras looked at him earnestly, then returned to her stall.

"She's very nice to us, isn't she, Mother?" he asked Romantic Myth.

"Yes, Freddie, she is."

"She's very wise too," he added.

His mother looked at him tenderly. She knew that for all his naïveté, this experience had made him a bit wiser as well. It pleased her to see him come to such a realization.

"Now you know why she is my best friend," Romantic Myth replied.

CHAPTER FIVE

The Longest Night

As THE SUMMER DAYS grew hotter, the once green hills turned pale yellow. The sun beat down on the pasture from late morning through mid-afternoon, when a cool breeze blew up the river from the sea. Then the eucalyptus trees rustled with cool relief and the birds once again started to sing, as another hot day soon became only a memory.

These late summer days were much the same for little Freddie. At six o'clock in the morning he was fed. He would nap most of the day, enjoying the sunshine. In the late afternoon he was fed again and then turned out to run in the pasture with his mother. He liked that part of the day best, and his owners seemed to like it, too. They would lean against the fence, laughing with amusement as he ran by. It seemed that the faster he ran, the more they smiled, as if sharing in his vigorous stride and the freedom he felt as he cantered.

"This one's going to be a runner," he heard them say.

"Mother, why did they say I was going to be a runner?" he asked Romantic Myth later.

"Because you show signs of being a good racehorse," she replied.

"What kind of signs?"

"A good racehorse has strong bones and straight legs. He is able to make quick turns, and start and stop whenever he wants. Most of all he likes to run," she replied.

This made Freddie happy. He wanted to be a great racehorse and felt proud to be admired by his owners.

"I love to run, Mother!" he exclaimed, and took off in a cloud of dust to the other side of the field.

When he had had enough exercise, he was haltered. They would walk a short way, with his mother nearby, and then stop. Freddie was praised if he walked at their side and stopped when he was asked. When the lessons were finished he was returned to his stall and given a handful of sweet feed.

One evening after feeding, Romantic Myth began to pace from one side of the stall to the other and groan in a low, strained voice. Freddie watched her anxiously, waiting for her to stop so that he could lie down and go to sleep, but she did not. Soon she was pawing the ground with her front hoof.

"Are you OK, Mother?" Freddie asked.

Romantic Myth did not answer. She paced irritably around the stall.

"Mother, are you all right?" he asked again.

Her face was strained and her eyes had lost their sparkle. "Yes," she said, trying not to worry her foal. "My stomach hurts, but I'm sure I will be fine in a little while."

As the sky grew darker and the stars of the Milky Way glittered above, Romantic Myth became worse. She walked about as much as she could until it no longer eased her pain. Finally, she lay down and began to thrash from one side to the other. Freddie watched her, in anguish, unable to help. Every time he tried to speak to her she did not answer. He was so frustrated at his helplessness that he started to cry.

"What's wrong with my mother?" he asked Mardi Gras, who was standing at the side of the stall. She had been there watching over her friend since the evening began.

"She is very sick, Freddie," Mardi Gras said seriously.

"It looks like it hurts so bad! I don't want her to hurt anymore."

"There is nothing we can do," Mardi Gras answered. "We just have to wait for the sun to come up. When they come to feed us they will see that she needs help."

"But it won't be morning for so long." The little colt's voice was heavy with worry.

Mardi Gras knew how sick Romantic Myth was and that she needed to rest until the veterinarian could be called. She wanted to keep Romantic Myth calm and Freddie quiet. She decided it was best to tell little Freddie the truth about his mother's illness. She hoped it would give him the courage he needed to stay by his mother's side and help her through the long night ahead.

"Freddie," Mardi Gras began, "I've seen horses sick like this before. It is something called colic."

Freddie listened closely. "Will she get better?"

Mardi Gras was silent for a moment. Her look was grave.

"Colic is very serious. Sometimes a horse can get better with help from a doctor and medicine, but sometimes nothing can help and the horse does not survive."

Freddie was stunned. It was as if the blood in his veins had turned to ice water. He shivered at the thought of his mother dying.

"But I don't want her to die," he said with tears running down his face.

Mardi Gras was sympathetic. Romantic Myth was so close to her. It was hard to see her suffer.

"The best thing you can do for your mother is to let her rest. Stay by me and we'll wait together for sunrise. Then the doctor will help her."

Romantic Myth was worse with each passing minute. She rolled from one side to the other to ease the pain. Then, out of utter exhaustion she collapsed, lying on her side and scarcely breathing.

The night seemed to last forever. The cold hours fueled the fears of the others who could only watch helplessly. Finally, thin rays of sunlight peeked over the hills. The roosters crowed as beams of light turned the once black sky to shades of royal blue.

When their owner came to feed it was plain to see the seriousness of Romantic Myth's condition. The sick horse was brought to her feet.

"Call the vet! Right away! Romantic Myth is sick!" she yelled.

When the veterinarian arrived he gave the mare some medicine for pain. Soon she appeared to be feeling better.

After a while, the vet finished his work and left, and everyone was fed their ration of hay except Romantic Myth. Instead, they took her out in the pasture and walked her slowly.

Since the vet was gone, Freddie was sure that his mother was getting better. He munched his hay relieved that he and Romantic Myth would be able to spend yet another day together. Then out of the corner of his eye he saw his mother fall to the ground.

"Mother!"

The lady clapped her hands to get her to stand. Romantic Myth stumbled to her feet, but the pain had returned.

Freddie was so preoccupied with Romantic Myth's condition that he did not notice as a trailer pulled up alongside the pasture. He and his mother were led to it. Romantic Myth stepped in, but Freddie refused to move. The last time he rode in a trailer it took him away from his friends. He did not want the same thing to happen again.

Before he could resist he was lifted inside and they were on their way. His mother leaned to one side and looked as if she wanted to drop. She had not spoken to him since the night before, and he knew that her silence meant she was too weak to talk. Freddie wished Mardi Gras could have come along. He was frightened.

The truck took them through a large valley where pastures with horses lined both sides of the road. At first Freddie thought they might be going back to the farm where he was born, but when they stopped he did not recognize the new place.

Romantic Myth and the colt were taken into a large room where she was examined. The mare was growing weaker with each minute that passed. Freddie stood quietly with his head held high, the way he had been taught. He heard a nurse say that he had very good manners. They had been brought to an equine hospital.

Soon they were taken to a stall inside the building. There was a mare and another foal next to them. He and Freddie looked at each other for a long time through a wire-mesh window that separated the stalls.

"Who is your father?" the little foal in the next stall finally asked.

Freddie paused a moment. He had never thought about it, and his mother had never told him. He wondered if foals are supposed to know who their fathers are. It must not have been important or Romantic Myth would have told him before.

"Gee, I don't know," Freddie answered.

"Well, my father is Rich Victory. He won the Kentucky Derby," the foal said proudly.

"What's the Kentucky Derby?" little Freddie asked.

The other colt looked at him in surprise. "The Kentucky Derby is the greatest race in the world—I think," he said, pondering his statement. "It is a long race run the first Saturday each May. They call it the 'Run for the Roses,' because if you win, a blanket of red roses is placed across your withers. Only great horses win the Kentucky Derby."

"Then that is the race I want to win," replied little Freddie confidently. "Because I want to be the greatest racehorse in the world."

"Me, too," the colt agreed.

"Then we can be friends, because someday we will probably race against each other at the Kentucky Derby."

"OK. What is your name?"

"My name is Freddie. What's yours?"

"My name is Rich Minute. That is because my father was Rich Victory and my mother is Classic Minute. They do that sometimes, take a name from the father and mother to name their foal."

"Well, I don't think they did that when they thought of my name because my mother's name is Romantic Myth. . . . "

Suddenly, Freddie remembered that she was very sick. He turned to see that she was lying on the floor of the stall, her head resting on the lap of their owner.

"My mother is sick. She has colic, that's why we're here."

Rich Minute peered through the window. His curious stare changed to concern as he lowered his ears.

"My mother is sick, too, but she's not that sick. She just tried to jump a wall and cut her leg."

"Will she be all right?" Freddie asked.

"Yes, we're going home tomorrow," he replied.

"Well, I hope we can go home soon. Maybe I should try to get her up. She might feel better."

Little Freddie went to his mother's side. He watched her, wondering if he could do anything to make her feel better.

"Mother, let's practice walking around like we do when we are in the pasture," he said anxiously.

Romantic Myth did not reply.

"Come on, Mother, stand up. I don't like to see you feeling so bad!"

Again, she said nothing.

"Please, Mother!" he tried to get her attention by nudging

her with his front leg. "It would really be fun to practice walking around the stall. I promise to be very good and not walk ahead of you. Please, you have to get up."

Romantic Myth lay motionless. Freddie nudged her again, but she did not even know he was there. Finally, he gave up and lay down beside her, trying to comfort her the same way she always comforted him. There was nothing else he could do.

They lay together on the stall floor quietly, until the silence was broken when a man entered and startled Freddie to his feet. He thought for sure he was there to take his mother, but to his surprise the man came to him. He held him firmly by the halter, and Freddie felt a slight prick in his neck. He had been given a shot.

At first he did not feel any different, then he began to get very sleepy. His legs were like jelly and everyone appeared to be moving in slow motion. Two more attendants came in and took Romantic Myth out of the stall. Other than when she was bred, Freddie had never been separated from his mother, and he wanted to follow but his legs would not move. He tried to call to her, but he was too tired to make any sound. He was alone for the first time in his young life. He stood in the middle of the large, lonely stall. This was worse than leaving Patches and Thunderball.

Gradually, the little colt lowered himself to the floor and fell into a deep sleep, dreaming all the while that his mother was not sick and had never left.

When he awoke she still had not returned, but he at least felt like himself again. He jumped to his feet and ran to the stall door to look for her.

"Mother!" he called as loud as he could. "Mother, where are you?"

He listened for an answer.

"Mother!" he called again. "Mother, please answer, I want to come to you."

Freddie could feel himself getting more and more upset each time she did not answer. He paced the stall, calling to her every few minutes, but she still did not call back.

The mare in the next stall felt sorry for Freddie. She knew how hard it was for a foal to be left alone.

"Don't worry, your mother will come back when she is better," she said comfortingly.

He looked back at her with sadness in his eyes. "But, when will she be better?" he pleaded. "I miss her. She would get better if we were together."

"I know," the mare replied. "If it were possible, I'm sure she'd rather have you with her too. Mothers miss their foals as much as the foals miss their mothers."

Little Freddie went to the door and called Romantic Myth again, and this time she called back. He could hear her familiar walk coming down the hall, and he waited anxiously for her to round the corner.

When she entered the stall he could see that she was frail and washy. Her face showed the strain of enduring many hours of pain with little sleep.

"Mother, are you all right now?" he asked.

"Yes, son, I am fine."

She nuzzled her little foal, happy to be with him again.

Freddie's appetite returned immediately. When he went to

nurse, he noticed her stomach had a long cut down the center with stitches.

"Don't worry," she said. "It will heal soon enough."

When he had finished nursing he felt very sleepy. All of the excitement and worry had made him tired. He lay down in the center of the stall and Romantic Myth lay down beside him.

"Mother, I'm glad you're better," he said rubbing his sleepy eyes. "I was so frightened when they took you away. I was afraid that you would never come back, and I would be alone for the rest of my life."

Romantic Myth pressed the side of her face against his forehead. "Right now you are too young to be by yourself, but someday you won't be. There will come a time when you are old enough to get along without me."

Freddie looked at her, puzzled. "But Mother, I don't want to be without you. I love you and I want us to always be together," he said seriously.

"I love you, too. That's why it is important for me to teach you everything I can while we are together. I want you to have a good life, even if I am not there to share it with you," she said, kissing the little colt softly.

"Does this mean you will be leaving me again?"

"When it is the right time, you will be on your own. You will go off to pursue your dreams. All I can do is teach you what I can to help you to get everything out of life that you want," she said quietly. "But for now, we are still together. When the time comes for us to be apart, you will understand what I mean."

"I will?"

"Yes," she said reassuringly. "Freddie?"

"Yes, Mother?"

"You were very brave today."

"Really?"

"Yes, and I'm very proud of you." Romantic Myth saw the pride swell in the young colt's eyes.

"I want you to be proud of me," he replied.

"I am. Rest now, we've had a very long day," she said. Freddie laid his head next to hers and they fell fast asleep.

CHAPTER SIX

Back to the Farm

WHEN ROMANTIC MYTH RECOVERED they did not go back to their owners' house. Instead, they went back to the farm where Freddie was born. They were happy to be with their friends again, and even the old nag Silverblue seemed happy that they had returned.

The days were very warm, and Freddie loved the long, waning hours of sunshine and the balmy late summer nights. He and Thunderball spent each afternoon playing in the pasture, and it seemed to Freddie as though he had never left.

"I'll bet I can beat you to that fence!" Thunderball challenged one day.

"I'll bet you can't!" Freddie replied as he bolted away, trying to get a head start.

Each colt ran his fastest. The two were of equal size, and shared the same competitive spirit. They were easily the fastest colts in the pasture, and the proudest.

Thunderball and Freddie were dead even as they passed the old oak tree, the halfway point to the fence. Freddie fixed

his sight on his destination, striding out farther with every step. Thunderball quickened the pace as they neared the fence. Freddie kept up, staying ahead of Thunderball by only a neck to finish first.

They were exhausted, but the two foals whinnied and stood on their hind legs wrestling with each other.

"I thought you were going to beat me!" Freddie said.

"So did I!" Thunderball laughed. "Next time I will."

Freddie looked up to respond to Thunderball's declaration, and found himself eye to eye with the great stallion Royal Exile. Even though they were separated by a fence, the foal wanted to step away, but he was trapped in the stoic gaze of the massive horse.

"Whose foal are you?" he asked in an intimidating voice.

For a moment Freddie could not get the words out of his mouth to answer.

"Whose foal are you?" the stallion asked again.

"I-I'm Freddie, my mother is Romantic Myth," he stammered.

The stallion eyed little Freddie up and down, sizing him up.

Freddie stood frozen in his tracks. He was in awe of the stallion. He had heard the stories of his great racing career, how he had won almost every race he had entered. The mares in the pasture whispered amongst themselves about how handsome he was when he passed by the pasture.

Once Freddie saw him when he was turned out for his daily exercise and was amazed at how fast Royal Exile could run. He was a portrait of dignity, muscles rippling and hooves thundering across the ground. His eyes had the look of an eagle, a look that could pierce straight through anything he gazed upon.

"I know your mother. You don't look much like her though. Do you know who your sire is?" Royal Exile asked.

Freddie looked at the ground. He had forgotten to ask his mother who his father was when the question first arose at the hospital. It did not seem so important at the time. Now he wished he had remembered to ask her, because he felt very foolish not knowing.

"I don't know," Freddie answered, shamefully bowing his head.

The stallion cast a disapproving gaze.

"Don't bow your head!" he said impatiently. "A racehorse should be proud and confident. His head should never hang down."

At his admonishment the little colt immediately stood at attention, with his head up and his chest out.

"That's better," he stated. "You should know who your father is. Ask your mother. Tell her that Royal Exile thinks you should know."

He stepped to the other side of Freddie to look at him from a different angle.

"How old are you?"

"I'm five months old."

"You run very fast for your age. Your stride will be long, take advantage of that. Remember to keep your head up and stretch it out as far as you can when you run. That will keep you in front when a race comes down to the wire. Do you understand?"

Little Freddie nodded. He felt himself swell with pride to

hear Royal Exile say he was a fast runner.

"Now, go back to your mother and tell her what I have said."

The stallion watched as Freddie bolted across the pasture toward the herd.

The two colts ran faster this time, partly out of fear and partly out of excitement that they had actually spoken to the stallion.

When they reached the others they were breathless and lathered with sweat. Each struggled to speak first.

"He talked . . . " little Freddie stammered. They were the only words he could utter between breaths.

"Royal Exile talked to Freddie!" Thunderball finished the sentence.

Romantic Myth smiled at the excited foals. "And what did he say?" she asked.

Freddie took a big gulp of air. "He said . . . "

"He said that he runs very fast, and that he doesn't look like you at all," Thunderball interrupted.

"He told me . . . " Freddie tried to speak again.

"He told him never to bow his head, that's what he said!" interjected Thunderball.

"Which one of you did he speak to?" Silverblue asked.

"Well, he talked to Freddie," Thunderball admitted. "Boy, I sure thought he was gonna get mad because we were there. He didn't though, at least I don't think he was mad."

"I don't know," Freddie replied finally, having caught his wind. "I don't think he was mad either. I sure am glad about that!"

The two mares were amused at the naïveté of their colts.

The colts had no idea that someday they would be just like Royal Exile, handsome and robust, and he would not seem as awesome.

Little Freddie stood at his mother's side for a long time trying to regain his composure. When he had calmed down enough to speak, he remembered what he wanted to ask.

"Mother, who is my sire?"

"Why do you ask, Freddie?"

He thought a moment. "Well, because twice I was asked who my father was and I don't even know. Once was when you were at the hospital. Rich Minute asked me. He knew who his father was. He said his father had won the Kentucky Derby. I didn't know if my father had won any races because I don't even know his name.

"Then today, Royal Exile asked me again. I felt so foolish because I couldn't answer. He said to tell you that I should know who my father is."

"I see," his mother replied. "Well, the next time you are asked who your sire is, tell them that it is Royal Exile."

"Royal Exile? He is my sire?"

"Why yes, Freddie."

"It's . . . it's just that he was such a great racehorse."

"Yes he was. I think you look very much like him. You should be proud to have such a noble sire."

The little colt stood very tall.

"Your father was a great horse, and his father was a great horse, too. Remember that when you race, and it will help you to have the confidence and desire to do your best."

"Why is that?"

"Because competition can be difficult," she continued. "A

real race can be much harder than beating Thunderball to the fence. When you run at the track it will be against horses who are as fast as you, and sometimes faster. You can still beat them if you believe in yourself. Always believe that you can win, and try your hardest. Even when others are ahead it will give you heart. That is what makes a great champion."

Freddie was quiet a moment.

"It will be much clearer when you race. You'll understand what heart and confidence really are."

"When will I run my first race?"

His mother looked at him with a hint of sadness in her eyes. She knew that her colt was getting old enough to be on his own, he was growing up so quickly. For as much as she loved him, she knew that out of love she had to let him go someday to find his own way in life. That was what growing up was all about.

"It will be soon enough, Freddie. It will be soon enough," she said, quietly nuzzling him.

As the days grew shorter the chilly autumn wind rustled through the trees. The leaves began to fall, Orion arose each night from the east, and the foals in the pasture were gradually weaned from their mothers. They were separated one at a time, so as not to create too much of a disturbance in the herd.

Little Freddie was standing with Romantic Myth near the oak tree. He was watching a nest of birds, thinking of when they were first born. They had had no feathers at all, and waited impatiently for their mother to bring food. Now, they were fully feathered and could find their own food.

Thunderball was at the end of the pasture. He had been separated from Silverblue the day before and was very dejected. He was exhausted from running the pasture fence calling to her throughout the night. His calls were unanswered. Although he was calm now, he was sad alone.

"Mother, will Thunderball ever feel better?" Freddie asked.

"Yes, after a while it won't seem so lonely. He'll have the other foals to keep him company, like you," she reassured Freddie.

She knew that the time was getting very close for her and Freddie to be separated as well. She wanted to give her colt all the reassurance she could before that time came.

"Do you remember the first time we rode in a trailer together?" she asked.

"Yes, and we went to our owners' house and you saw Mardi Gras again," he answered.

"That's right," Romantic Myth nodded. "Do you remember how you were very lonely for Thunderball because you had to leave him?"

"Uh-huh," Freddie nodded.

"You thought that you would never see him again, and I told you that when you care for someone very much that caring survives separation. And even if you never see them again, the love you feel is always there."

"Yes, I remember, because then you saw Mardi Gras and you were both happy to see each other," Freddie replied.

Romantic Myth nuzzled her colt very close to her. She loved him, and she knew that no matter what happened the bond between a mother and foal could never be broken, even if they were never together again. It would be as hard for her to leave as it would be for him. Yet she understood that it was nature's way, and it was time for her colt to be on his own.

"Don't you ever forget that experience, Freddie. It will help you to understand what it is to be independent," she said with a touch of sorrow in her kind eyes.

Freddie looked at her. She was so serious it made him think something was wrong.

"Why are you telling me this?"

"Because it is important that you know these things," Romantic Myth smiled, trying to hide the sadness that she felt. "I love you very much, and I want you always to be happy."

Freddie smiled back. "I love you, too," he said with shining eyes.

"Now go play with Thunderball. It will be feeding time soon and I think he would like the company."

Freddie ran over to Thunderball, who was staring at the ground.

"Come on Thunderball, I'll race you to the fence," little Freddie said, hoping to cheer him up.

"No, I don't feel very much like running," he replied.

Freddie stood a moment trying to think of something to say that would make him feel better.

"Well, gee, maybe we could walk over to the other side of that hill. I found some dandelions growing there—we could share them," he offered.

Thunderball shook his head. He didn't seem to want to do anything at all. Just then two men came into the pasture. They had a lead rope for one of the horses. Freddie watched them cross the field and stop at Romantic Myth. They hooked the rope to her halter and began to walk toward the pasture gate. Freddie raced across the field to reach them, but by the time he got to the gate it had already been closed behind them.

"Mother, where are you going?" he asked, upset that he was not allowed to follow.

She looked at him over the shoulder of the man leading her down the road toward a truck and trailer.

"You be a good boy, Freddie, and try to remember everything I've told you. I know you will be a great racehorse someday, and I will be very proud of you," she said.

Freddie was running along the side of the fence trying to keep up with her.

"Mother, don't go without me. I want to go," Freddie said frantically.

"I know, but you can't go with me this time. I love you, Freddie, don't forget that," she said sorrowfully, bowing her head to hide her tears.

Freddie had reached the end of the pasture and was unable to follow her any farther. He watched as they loaded her in the trailer and closed the door.

"I love you too, Mother!" he yelled.

She turned, silently acknowledging what he had said. She looked back at him until the trailer turned onto the main highway. Freddie watched the truck drive away until it disappeared into the distance. He was alone, and now he understood what his mother had been trying to tell him.

CHAPTER SEVEN

On His Own

FREDDIE'S FIRST WINTER BEGAN lonely and wet. It seemed that as soon as Romantic Myth left it rained for days on end.

The first days were the hardest. He did not feel like playing with his friends and had no appetite. All he wanted was to be with his mother again. The cold, damp nights made the little colt feel even more alone. He would huddle next to the other foals in the herd for warmth, their backs to the wind.

When the sky roared with thunder and flashed with lightning, he would close his eyes and think about the talks he and Romantic Myth used to have. She had often told him of her experiences while at the racetrack, how there were many times when she had felt frightened of the unknown, but she would gather her confidence and face her fears. And it always seemed that her imagination made them worse than they really were. It made him feel better to think of the courage his mother had shown when she was a racehorse. Little Freddie wanted to be that brave.

As the weeks went by he eventually missed her less and less. Although he could never replace the special love the two of them had shared, it was hard not to enjoy the camaraderie of the other colts. They had all been weaned by the time the trees were barren of autumn's colors, and the once small birds in the oak tree had long since been able to fly on their own.

Thunderball and Freddie were closer than ever before. Thunderball was a fast, muscular horse that Freddie liked to challenge to race. Unlike some of the other colts, he was spirited enough to be fast, but calm enough to still be friendly. The old nag Silverblue had taken great pains to teach him to be an honest competitor, and her efforts had not been in vain.

One morning after they had finished their hay, Patches came running to Freddie and Thunderball, excited and out of breath. She scurried to the top board of the fence so that she was eye level with the colts.

"Someone new is coming today. They're bringing him right now, look!" she pointed.

Freddie and Thunderball looked up the road.

"Hey Freddie, they sure are bringing someone new. Do you think they'll put him in with us?" Thunderball asked.

Freddie looked up the narrow road alongside the pasture and saw a grey colt led by the stablehand. His steps were short and tense, as if he were prancing in place. His neck was bowed and the whites of his eyes showed as they darted from one place to another. He looked skittish, as if he did not recognize his surroundings. Freddie had never seen him before.

"Gee, I don't know. It looks like it," he replied. "He sure doesn't look like he's happy to be here."

The stablehand opened the gate and walked the excited colt into the pasture. The rest of the herd watched curiously, wondering who the newcomer was.

The stablehand waited until he was sure the herd was calm, then he unsnapped the lead rope and turned the horse loose.

Unsure of himself, he approached the others slowly. It was always difficult for newcomers, because they were often challenged by the others to test their competitiveness and resolve. Acceptance was not easy. First this horse had to earn the respect of the herd before he was really considered a part of the group.

As he came closer, little Freddie could see that he was sweating so much that his chest was lathered. He seemed more unsure of himself the closer he came.

"Who are you?" Revolver asked first. He was by far the biggest one in the herd and would always bully the other horses at feeding time. If there was going to be a fight, Revolver would be in the middle of it.

"My name is Gallant Grey," he answered. "My dam is Shadow Grey, and my sire is Gallant Light, so they call me Gallant Grey."

"What's a dam and a sire?" Thunderball whispered to Freddie.

"A dam is a mother, and a sire is a father," Freddie answered.

"Oh. Why didn't he just say that?"

Freddie shrugged. "I don't know. Maybe where he came

from that's what they call a mother and father. He acts like he has never been alone before."

"So, where are you from?" Revolver asked. Gallant Grey approached him cautiously since he was the only one who had spoken so far.

"I came from Willow Creek, it's a farm just up the road. I know it isn't very far because I only rode in the trailer for a short time," he said politely. "Besides, it can't be that far because my mother is still there, and I'll have to be brought home before feeding time."

Revolver scoffed at his naïveté.

"Yeah—well, I wouldn't count on that. They brought you here because you're not going to be taken back to her. You're going to be weaned like all the rest of us," he said coldly.

"You don't have to be so mean, Revolver," Patches hissed. She had taken a seat between Freddie and Thunderball and was watching curiously, waiting to find out who the new colt was.

"Oh shut up, you stupid cat," Revolver grumbled as he turned back to Gallant Grey.

The grey colt stared back at him in disbelief. "That's not true! I will be going back very soon. They wouldn't take me away from my mother," he protested.

"Oh yeah? You're wrong. All of us were taken away from our mothers about a month ago. Why did they wait so long to wean you? What are you, a mama's boy or something?" Revolver butted the colt with his head.

"Don't! I am not a mama's boy, but I know that she wouldn't let them take me away."

Revolver smirked. He was taking particular pleasure in intimidating the new colt.

"Well she did," Revolver shoved him again.

"Stop it!" Gallant Grey was trying to hold his ground without looking too frightened. Unfortunately, his fear was far too apparent to the combative Revolver. The more Revolver pushed him, the more upset he became until he could no longer stand the taunting and bolted to a gate at the other end of the pasture, next to the broodmares.

Revolver chased the scared little colt until he was cornered. He shoved him again and Gallant Grey fell against the gate, cutting his shoulder. He cried out partly from pain, and partly from the desperate feeling he had at the news that he would not be returned to his mother.

"Look, he's scared!" Revolver taunted. A couple of the other colts jeered and made the newcomer's legs begin to quiver.

"I'm not scared," he said, trying to stand his ground.

"Sure he is!" first one taunted, and then the others.

Little Freddie was watching with mixed emotions. There were bound to be fights in the herd, but this seemed particularly cruel. It was hard enough to be separated from your mother for the first time, or to be the new horse in the pasture, but to face both prospects at once would be a frightening test for even the bravest foal. He did not like the way Revolver always picked on others and it made him angry to see this relentless pursuit. He thought of the time that Grant had tried to fight with him. Mardi Gras prevented him from being hurt in an unfair match. She had said that someday he might have to discern what was fair on his own.

"I wish Revolver wouldn't be this way," Patches said. "It's so unfair the way they're acting. I don't think the grey has got a chance against the three of them."

Gallant Grey reared and kicked at Revolver and the other two yearlings, but three against one was too much for him. Every time he faced one, the others would kick him in the ribs and throw him off balance. Freddie knew that this was the time Mardi Gras had spoken of. He ran to the aid of Gallant Grey, and Thunderball followed. They came to a halt just in front of him.

"Get out of here, you two. We're just having a little fun," Revolver snapped.

Freddie looked back defiantly. "What you are doing isn't fair—it's three against one."

"So what are you going to do, fight for him?" Revolver asked sarcastically.

"No," Thunderball replied, "we're going to make it even— three against three."

Freddie and Thunderball stood between Revolver and Gallant Grey, who was bleeding from his shoulder.

Revolver was quiet, silently sizing up the situation. It was one thing to rough up a newcomer and have a little bit of fun showing how tough he could be, but it was another thing to start a fight with someone whose strength and speed were equal to his own. While Revolver was not a close friend with either Freddie or Thunderball, he knew that they were not intimidated by him. He also knew that Freddie was right, and he didn't want to become unpopular with the others.

"Why do you want to stick up for a mama's boy like him? Look at him, he's crying 'cause he wants to go back to his mother. He doesn't even know how to fight." Revolver was trying to justify his actions.

"We were all scared the first time we were away from our mothers. I don't think he's any different from the rest of us, except that he's new and has no friends yet. Just ease up on the guy."

"We're just having a little fun," Revolver grumbled.

"Hurting others isn't fun," Thunderball stated. "You wouldn't like it, so leave him alone."

Freddie and Thunderball stared at Revolver with unbending determination. Their minds were made up; Revolver would have to leave Gallant Grey alone, at least for now.

"Well," Revolver said, indignantly. "He's not worth it anyway, he's too much of a sissy to fight back. Come on guys, let's go."

Little Freddie and Thunderball watched Revolver and his friends as they walked back to the herd. When they were sure the three were not coming back, they relaxed and turned to their new friend.

"Hi, I'm Freddie, and this is Thunderball," he greeted the colt.

"And I'm Patches," the cat quickly added as she joined them.

"Hi," Gallant Grey said, rubbing the sweat from his brow onto his foreleg. "Thanks for the help."

"Oh sure," Thunderball replied. "Revolver really isn't a bad guy, he just likes to see who is afraid of him. If you ever challenge him alone, he usually backs down anyway."

"Is it true what he said about me never seeing my mother again?" Gallant Grey asked.

Both colts could see the concern in his eyes. He wanted them to say that it was not true, that he would return to

Willow Creek when feeding time came, but they could not.

The truth was that he would probably never see his mother again. Maybe none of them would, and they would have to remember them by the few short months they had together when they had never strayed more than a few yards from their mothers' sides.

"Yes," Freddie said quietly. "It's time for you to be weaned. That's what happens when you're old enough to be on your own. It means you're growing up."

"I've heard some horses say that they did see their mothers again after they were all grown up," Thunderball added. "So I wouldn't say that you'll never see her again, but maybe you'll have to wait a little while, that's all."

Gallant Grey bowed his head. Freddie felt bad for him because he could remember the loneliness he felt the first day away from Romantic Myth. He wished there was something he could do to lift his spirits, but he knew that learning to be independent was not something anyone could do for you.

"It'll be OK," little Freddie comforted. "We've been weaned and we made it all right. It's lonely for a while, but it gets better."

"Sure it does," Patches encouraged. "I don't have a mother, but I have a lot of friends here."

"Yeah," Thunderball agreed. "Pretty soon you'll feel like running and playing like everyone else."

The new colt's head was still lowered. "I don't think so," he said sadly. "I'll miss my mother too much."

Freddie thought back to what the mare in the next stall had told him when he was separated from Romantic Myth during her surgery. "Your mom will miss you too, but she knows that it's time for you to grow up. Come on, we'll introduce you to everyone else. They're not all like Revolver. Most of them are pretty nice."

"Yeah, and you can hang around with us," added Thunderball.

The two colts led their new friend to the other side of the pasture. They were followed by Patches, who with her usual lighthearted step jumped at the shadow of a bird passing overhead.

CHAPTER EIGHT

As a Yearling

THE SEASONS HAD GONE full circle and little Freddie was almost completely grown. The passing months had allowed his grace and ability to mature, and he had grown to be a tall, handsome chestnut colt. It was summer once again. The days were soothing and lazy, interrupted only by an occasional pestering fly.

One day the farm workers came to the pasture, haltered each of the colts, and took them each to a barn stall. Even though they were together, it was strange to be inside and isolated from the herd. Freddie was next to Thunderball. It made him feel better to talk to him through the window between their stalls.

"Thunderball?"

"Yes, Freddie?"

"Why do you suppose we're here?" Freddie asked.

Thunderball was quiet for a moment. He was an intelligent colt and Freddie admired his even temperament. Freddie was silent, waiting for him to answer. Thunderball looked

around the barn. He found these surroundings very bewildering.

"It could be anything, I suppose. Maybe they are about to
take us somewhere else to live, like they did with our mothers when we were weaned."

Freddie thought out loud, "I don't think that's it. They took
all of us out of the pasture at once. They took our mothers
away one at a time. It seems like there would be too many of
us to take all at once."

"Maybe we are all going to be shod, or see the vet," Thunderball suggested.

"When the farrier or the vet comes, they usually go out to
the pasture."

Thunderball shrugged. "I guess if we just wait we'll find
out soon enough. I hope we don't have to stay inside for very
long. I would rather be out in the sunshine."

The next morning Freddie recognized his owners coming
through the barn door. He was glad to see them. It helped to
have someone familiar in a strange place.

They walked up to his stall, said hello, and gave him a pat
on the neck. Then they took a soft brush and began to brush
him, starting first at his withers, then working down to his
tail. What Freddie did not notice was that each of the colts in
the barn had someone in his stall doing the very same thing.

After a few moments they stopped brushing him. One of
them reached down and picked up first one of his hooves and
then the other three until all had been cleaned.

"There, that's enough for today," one said, and then they
said goodbye.

They came back the next morning and the next, and did

the same thing. Then one morning they arrived with a strange-looking halter that had a shiny piece of metal at one end.

One of them patted his neck softly. "Steady now, boy. It's time you learned to be bridled. This will feel awkward, but won't hurt at all."

Gently the bridle was slipped over his head. The bit was attached to the bridle on one end so that it dangled beneath Freddie's chin. They took the bit, brought it to Freddie's lips, and slipped it into his mouth. Freddie began to chomp on it until he eventually got used to the feeling.

"That's a good boy." They handed him a piece of apple as a reward for taking the bit so agreeably.

Freddie was surprised to find that he could eat with the bit in his mouth. He finished the apple and nuzzled them for more.

They stayed with him for a while longer, then took the bit and bridle off and left for the day.

This routine lasted a few days. Freddie was bridled, then after he was used to that, a saddle pad was placed on his back. This was far more unnerving than taking a bit. He stood very rigid while his owners waited for him to adjust to having weight on his back for the first time. When he relaxed a little the saddle was placed in the center of his back. It was heavier than the pad.

Slowly they walked him around the stall the same way they had walked him in the pasture the year before when he was learning to wear a halter. It reminded him of the days he and Romantic Myth were together, and his owners would visit with them. He wondered how she was. Little could he know that by this time she had another young foal to care for who was as small as Freddie had been only a year ago. So much had happened in that time.

He was led around the stall three or four more times, then unsaddled. He had finished his lesson for this day.

Little by little the cinch around his middle was tightened a notch at a time, until it was secure enough for him to carry a rider. Within a week his owner was able to sit in the saddle and guide him with the reins. As he walked he felt more sure of himself with each step he took.

That evening Freddie asked his stablemate, "Thunderball, do you like all this—the training, I mean?"

Thunderball pondered Freddie's question. "Well, it's all so new. Everyone is nice, but sometimes I'm not sure what I'm supposed to do."

Freddie nodded. "Me too. I think it's more fun to just run outside. This sure isn't like being in the pasture."

"Nope, it isn't. My mother told me that once we've started training there aren't many times when we're allowed to run free until we finish racing."

Freddie felt a bit saddened that the long lazy days in the sunshine had come to an end. He had always wanted to be a racehorse, but he longed for the days in the pasture when he had nothing more to do than play with his friends.

"Well Thunderball, I guess this is what we've been talking about since we were young," the colt said.

"Yep, Fred. We'll be racehorses sooner than you think," he replied.

Thunderball was right. Little Freddie was not so little anymore. He had done all that was asked of him while training.

Now, at two years old, he was strong enough to carry a rider at a full gallop with ease.

Soon, like the other colts he trained with, he took up a new residence at the racetrack. Thunderball was still his stablemate. They ran together in the morning and shared their experiences in the afternoon. But mostly they talked about the big day when they would run in their first race. And then that day came.

CHAPTER NINE

To the Track

LIKE EVERY OTHER MORNING, Freddie woke with the dawn and waited patiently to be fed and exercised. But he knew that he would be racing today, and was very excited and nervous to finally run. He tried to remember what Romantic Myth had told him about her racing days, but still didn't quite know what to expect. Today he was on his own, armed only with the many hours of hard work and training that had brought him this far.

He could hear the people as they filtered by the stables near the track entrance. These were familiar sounds, because he had been at the track for several weeks.

He liked to listen to the sounds from the grandstand. Even though he could not see the track, he knew when the horses were entering the homestretch and approaching the finish line by the cheering of the crowd. He hoped someday they would cheer like that for him.

"Hey, Freddie, did you know we're in the first race?" Thunderball asked.

Freddie shook his head. "No. Does it matter?"

Thunderball shrugged. "The big race is toward the end of the day. That's usually the race everyone comes to see. We're just beginners so they put us first. Nobody really knows us yet."

"Oh," Freddie paused. "Thunderball, are you nervous?"

Thunderball moved very close so that none of the other horses could hear what he was saying. "I guess so. I'd never admit it to anyone else. I know I can trust you not to tell anybody."

Freddie nodded. "I wouldn't tell anybody. I'm nervous too. I hope I remember what I'm supposed to do."

"You will," Thunderball reassured him. "Just do the best you can, that's all that's important. It'll be like when we raced each other in the pasture back at the farm."

"Yep, just like that. You know, Thunderball, sometimes I miss that. When I'm not too tired, that is." Freddie was quiet a moment. "Those were fun times."

"They sure were," Thunderball agreed. "I like thinking about those days. The funny thing is that all the horses we knew at the farm spent their time thinking about their racing days, and we're doing just the opposite. We're racing and thinking about the days in the pasture. I suppose someday we'll reminisce about our racing days, too."

"I suppose so," Freddie replied.

Jeb poked his head around the corner, catching the attention of the two colts. He was a gritty old golden retriever who, in his years as the unofficial barn foreman, had become all too familiar with the ups and downs of racing. He had been in the company of the greatest champions and the most sorrowful losers, but to him they were all the same. He knew that the finest blue-blooded Kentucky pedigree did not mean a thing. What really made a horse a winner was his attitude. Whether good or bad, it was what drove him to or discouraged him from reaching his goals.

As a stray pup he was taken in by the barn's trainer and had lived in the tack room ever since. An old saddle pad was used for his bed and battered tin buckets held his food and water. He walked with a limp because arthritis had long since stiffened his joints, and his muzzle was white with age. Still, his expression reflected a kindness beneath his outer gruffness.

"So you fellas are finally hitting the track?" he asked.

The two nodded.

"Well, I suppose the only thing I can tell ya is good luck," he said, scratching behind one ear. "A little luck never hurts."

"Thank you," Freddie answered politely. He looked up to the sight of his owners coming to his stall. They were dressed nicer than any other time they had come to visit. Today must be special for them too, he thought. The woman with the freckles patted him on the side of the neck and fed him a cube of sugar.

"See you in the paddock, buddy," the man said as they turned to leave.

"Attention, Horsemen," a deep voice sounded over the public address system. "This is the twenty-minute call for the first race. All horses running in the first race are due in the saddling area in twenty minutes."

That was their cue. Freddie and Thunderball looked down

the shed row to see their grooms approaching, bridles and halters in hand.

As the groom stepped into Freddie's stall, he took a long, careful look at Freddie. He wanted to be sure that his horse's coat was shiny and clean. He had to look his best for his first race.

Carefully, the groom put the bit in Freddie's mouth and slipped the bridle over his ears. Freddie lowered his head slightly so that the groom would not have to strain to make sure the bridle was straight before he fastened the noseband and bridle strap in place.

Taking a damp towel, he moved over Freddie's neck and shoulders in a circular motion, making sure his chestnut color had a brilliant sheen in the sunlight.

"Well, you're ready as you'll ever be, pal," his groom said, patting him on the forehead. "I want to take a picture with you in the winner's circle today, OK?"

Freddie rubbed his face against the groom's shoulder in agreement.

"Let's go," the trainer called to Freddie's and Thunderball's grooms.

Unsnapping the bar across the stall door, the groom led Freddie out into the barn aisle behind Thunderball.

A few of the other horses poked their heads out of their stalls as Freddie and Thunderball passed by.

"Good luck, Freddie; good luck, Thunderball," came their words of encouragement.

Freddie pranced down the road to the saddling barn. Every so often he would whinny excitedly to Thunderball, who in contrast was walking calmly and obediently by his groom's side.

As they reached the entrance to the saddling barn, the track veterinarian stopped to check each horse. It was important that each one running today be in good form.

Freddie waited impatiently for his turn, craning his neck forward so that he could see the paddock. It was a small oval area bordered by a white fence. In the center was green grass where all of the owners, trainers, and stablehands would stand when the horses were brought out for the rest of the people visiting the track that day to see.

He had been in the paddock gardens and the saddling area a few days before when he was taken there for practice. There was so much to look at. People in brightly colored clothes passed by, while birds hovered above the purple and yellow poppies, chirping to each other as they pecked at the spilled popcorn scattered on the ground.

Freddie was led to the fifth saddling stall, where his trainer brushed him down and put a black cloth on his back that had the number five in white on both sides.

When the saddle was in place, he was led from the barn to the paddock. He paraded past the crowd of people gathered at the rail to inspect the horses.

"That one looks good," he heard someone from the crowd say as he came to a halt in front of his trainer and the jockey who would ride him. Freddie could feel his excitement growing. He glanced at Thunderball, who was right in front of him. Thunderball looked back confidently.

"Just like racing in the pasture, Thunderball!" Freddie called.

"Yep, just like it!" Thunderball called back.

Freddie was glad he and Thunderball were racing in their first race together.

"Riders up!" the steward announced.

Freddie felt the sudden weight of the jockey on his back, and they followed the other horses through a tunnel under the grandstand, to the track. The lead ponies came alongside the runners to escort them to the starting gate.

As Freddie stepped into the afternoon sunlight and onto the racetrack for the first time, he was overwhelmed by the sound of the crowd. His nostrils flared and he could smell the aroma of hot dogs, popcorn, and cotton candy as he trotted in front of the grandstand. His ears were pricked attentively as he looked at the people who were looking back at him. Sensing that he was a little nervous, his jockey let Freddie loose from the lead horse to jog on his own. It felt good to warm up, and the more he ran the more relaxed he became.

The starting gate was at the farthest end of the track, away from the grandstand and noise. By the time he reached it he was filled with confidence.

Freddie caught sight of a bird perched on the rail at the opposite side of the gate. He thought of the nest of baby birds that lived in the oak tree in the pasture where he was born. He remembered watching them curiously when he was only days old. They were the first creatures he could remember seeing that were not horses. As he had grown up and learned to run, he watched the tiny fledglings learn to fly. Had they dreamed of flying like he dreamed of racing?

The bell sounded and the starting gate sprang open. The field of horses was on its way in a cloud of dust. Freddie was

caught off guard and started a half-step late. He sprinted to
the lead as fast as he could. His heart was pounding as he
galloped, fighting the pull of the bit that was telling him to
slow down. By the sound of the thundering hooves behind
him, he knew he was in first place by two or three lengths. He
could not bear to let another horse get in front of him. He
wanted to win this race too much.

The horses ran down the backstretch. As they neared the
far turn, the race was almost half over with Freddie still in
front. As they rounded the turn and came into the homestretch, the rest of the field pulled closer. Freddie put his ears
back and tried to increase his lead. Thunderball was able to
pull up to his hindquarters and other horses were right behind him.

The crowd cheered louder, and Freddie was struggling to
stay ahead of the pack. His legs ached and he felt the sting of
the jockey's whip. He tried to hold on as the finish line drew
near. He ran as hard as he could, only to watch Thunderball
and three other horses streak past him in a flash of lightning
speed. With a furlong to go, he could not catch them, as hard
as he tried. Finally, he crossed the wire with a bewildering
fifth place finish, just edging out a bay colt and a roan gelding. His body hurt from running so hard for such a distance.
Yet, it was nothing compared to the utter desolation of losing
his first race.

The jockey slowed Freddie gradually, then turned him back
to the unsaddling area at the side of the winner's circle. He
could hear the applause as Thunderball trotted back to the
grandstand. He was the winner.

Freddie came to a halt in front of his trainer. The jockey dismounted and unsaddled him.

"This one's got a lot of heart, but he's a little green," the jockey told the trainer.

Freddie's heart sank.

As he was led back to the barn, he looked behind him to see Thunderball in the winner's circle. His owners were proudly holding a bouquet of flowers and a trophy as the camera flashed their picture. Although Royal Exile had told him that a true champion never bowed his head, Freddie could not help but look to the ground as he slowly walked back to his stall.

CHAPTER TEN

Jeb's Kind Word

WHEN FREDDIE RETURNED to the barn he saw there was extra grain waiting for him. He sniffed it, but was too tired to eat. His legs felt like cement, and his stomach was in knots, but more than that, the feeling of being defeated was by far the most painful.

He looked in Thunderball's stall. He never dreamed that his friend would win and he would lose so terribly. He was unsure if Thunderball would still respect him, or if he himself would be able to put his injured pride aside and share in his friend's accomplishment.

"That's wrong," Freddie said aloud to himself. "Thunderball won fair and square, and you lost. Don't spoil his victory just because you came in fifth place."

"Who you talking to, boy?" Jeb asked, looking out from the tack room.

"No one, no one at all," Freddie answered quietly.

"What's the matter—you lose today?"

"Yes," Freddie said, bewildered.

Jeb took a step closer to him so that he might look him in the eye. "Well boy, I hate to tell you this, but this ain't gonna be the last time when the only thing you're first at is coming back to the barn. That's the way racing is, you win some and ten other horses lose some. But I'll tell you one thing, you can be flat-aching from running your heart out, but nothing is really hurt except your pride. You'll get another chance."

The dog did not wait for Freddie's reply. He just turned and went back to where he had been napping. As he lumbered off, he said without turning his head, "And from what I hear, you'll be winning soon enough."

Freddie stared after him thinking about what the wise old dog had said. Thunderball was his best friend because he was fair and kind, and he would have been happy for Freddie if the race had gone to him.

"This one's gonna be a champion!" he heard someone in the breezeway call out.

"Gonna be? He is one!" someone else exclaimed.

Freddie recognized the voice. It was Thunderball's groom. Thunderball was returning to his stall. For a moment Freddie felt very uncomfortable. He did not go to the stall door the way he normally did. Instead, he stood toward the back of his stall next to the feeder.

Immediately Thunderball came to the window between their stalls to see how Freddie was.

"Hey Freddie, you doing all right?" he asked.

"Sure," he replied without looking up.

Thunderball was quiet. He wanted to say something to ease the tension. He knew how disappointed Freddie must be.

"I don't know about you, but I don't think I've ever been so sore in my entire life. I thought if I hurt this bad from trying to catch up to you, you must be pretty sore from setting the pace."

Freddie lifted his head. "I'm pretty sore all right." He looked at Thunderball and thought to himself that his stablemate really did look exhausted. His eyes were dull from fatigue, and he was holding himself in an awkward way so as not to put all his weight on any one leg.

"You ran a good race," Freddie heard himself say. "You came by me like lightning. I didn't expect it at all, I thought I was going to win for sure."

Thunderball smiled. "I thought you were, too. You were in front the whole time until the stretch. I didn't think I could run anymore until I felt the whip. I was surprised I had anything left, to tell you the truth."

The two colts were weary and battle-worn. They looked at each other for a brief moment and then both began to laugh.

The uneasiness was gone. The uncertainty and nervousness were replaced with the camaraderie they had always shared. Now they understood how the horses at the breeding farm could talk about their racing days so affectionately with one another.

Freddie saw his owners coming and the tension returned. Would they still be as pleased with him as they were before the race? He had heard stories of other horses being sold when they did not win.

"Poor guy," one said. "He looks like he could use a vacation."

Freddie bent his head to take the apple offered to him.

"That's OK, we'll get 'em next time," the other encouraged.

He munched on the apple and nuzzled them both. He understood now that winning was not everything. Thunderball was still his friend and his owners still loved him. It was just as important to try his best even if he did not win, but now he was all the more determined to have another chance.

In the two weeks that followed Freddie and Thunderball settled back into their old routine of hectic morning workouts and idle afternoons in the barn. The difference now was the subject of conversation. They spoke of what had happened on the track, what they might have done differently, and what they would do better next time. Freddie watched the race over and over again in his mind from the first moment he was in the saddling area to the last instant when he crossed the finish line. Each time he thought how he could do it better. He would pay closer attention to his rider, concentrating on what he was asked to do. He would not be so overcome by the crowd in the paddock and grandstand. He would think of nothing else in the starting gate except the upcoming race.

During his workouts each morning he focused on the things he had mulled over with Thunderball until he was sure he would not make the same mistakes again.

When the time came for him to race again it was not against Thunderball, since he had already won. Instead, it was against horses like himself that had yet to win. He did not know any of the others, but as he was led onto the track he knew that he was an older and wiser competitor than he had been just two weeks before.

In the starting gate he stared straight ahead, settling in with his rider, trying to discern each movement he made.

When he left the gate he was unaware of the sound of the hooves around him or the crowd. He paced himself until the jockey let out the reins.

By the stretch run he had passed the rest of the field. This time he ran so well that his rider never used the whip. All he needed was a pat on the neck to hold fast to a smooth first-place finish, lengths ahead of the others.

Lathered with sweat and out of breath, Freddie entered the winner's circle for the first time. He felt the glory of standing with proud owners as his picture was taken and he was led off the track ahead of the other runners. He was a winner now.

When he returned to the barn he was just as tired as before, but this time he had a victory to ease the fatigue. As he approached his stall he saw Thunderball with his neck stretched as far out of the stall door as it would go. He had heard the sounds of the crowd and the announcer declare Freddie the winner, and he was excited to be the first to congratulate his stablemate.

"Hey Freddie, you won!" he called at the first sight of his friend.

"Yes, I did! I won!" Freddie called back.

This time he entered his stall with his head held high.

CHAPTER ELEVEN

Chance of a Lifetime

THE MORE FREDDIE RACED, the more he liked it. His life back at the farm seemed an eternity ago. He thought about Romantic Myth often, but he was too busy to spend much time reflecting on his days at the pasture. His thoughts were with racing. He looked forward to the hustle of the morning workouts, and had learned to love the eagerness he felt in the paddock before each race. He would walk past the people with his head held high, looking proud and ready to win.

Every race was different. His trainer said he had the heart of a champion. Each time he entered the winner's circle, his trainer said he won because he showed more desire than his opponents. Freddie had heart.

Freddie won almost every time he ran, but never when he raced against Thunderball. Thunderball was undefeated. The contests between them were furious duels. Each horse matched the other's pace down to the very last stride, but Thunderball always crossed the line first. Their friendship was not affected by competition. They respected each other as worthy opponents, and were able to separate competition from companionship.

After the cold winter months of racing on wet, sloppy tracks, spring was a welcome sight. The sun was brighter, the grass looked greener, and birds filled the air with beautiful songs to their mates. This was Freddie's third spring, and this year, like last year, he thought it was the prettiest one he had ever seen. Yet, this spring was different from the others, because with the sunshine and budding trees came talk of the Kentucky Derby.

At first Freddie had no idea that he could be a contender. He remembered that one day a few years ago when his mother was ill, he had talked about it with another colt whose name he could not remember. What he could remember, though, was that only the greatest racehorse won the Kentucky Derby.

One morning, while Freddie was being fed, a newspaper reporter asked his trainer whom he would be sending to the Derby. Freddie's trainer smiled. "My two best," he answered.

"Which two would that be?" asked the reporter.

"Why, these two, of course," the trainer replied, pointing at Thunderball and Freddie.

Freddie could hardly believe his ears. He and Thunderball would be running in the Kentucky Derby.

"Did you hear that, Thunderball? We're going to the Derby!" Freddie blurted out, unable to hide his excitement.

Thunderball, who had been munching on his feed, lifted his head in surprise. Hay was hanging from the sides of his mouth. "What did you say?"

"I said we're going to the Kentucky Derby!"

Thunderball took a step back and looked at Freddie suspiciously. It was too good to be true.

"Who told you that?" he asked.

"Nobody. I overheard our trainer talking to a reporter. The reporter asked him who he was sending to the race, and he pointed at us. Isn't it great?"

Thunderball was stunned. They had worked hard for this chance, but it was more than they could hope for. It was a dream come true. "Yes—yes, it is," he said in disbelief. "We're really going to the Derby? Now, you're sure that's what he said?"

"Uh-huh," Freddie nodded. "I guess we must be the best."

Thunderball looked at him hesitantly. He did not want this to go to their heads.

"Don't get overconfident. We still have a race Sunday that we better think about first. If we start thinking about the Derby and not about our next race, we could lose, and not go anywhere."

Just then a man with a camera came down the center aisle, accompanied by another man with a clipboard. They stopped in front of the two stalls.

"These are the Kentucky Derby entrants for this barn. I'll get their registration numbers and you get their picture," the man with the clipboard said.

The bright light of the camera flashed in Freddie's eyes and he knew that a dream was coming true.

CHAPTER TWELVE

The Old Rivalry

HEY, EITHER ONE OF YOU guys know a colt by the name of Revolver?" asked Jeb.

Freddie and Thunderball looked at each other.

"Yeah, we know him. Why?" Thunderball asked.

Jeb scratched his ear with his back leg.

"Well, he's down in barn 42. Says he knows you both and he's been sayin' how he can beat you. He used to do it all the time when you were kids. He's also been tellin' the boys down there that ya cheat. One of ya cuts the leader off so that the other one can take the lead. You'll be racin' against him today."

It had been a long time since the two had seen Revolver. Unfortunately, Revolver had not changed much, and he never forgot about his race with Freddie in the pasture. Apparently, he was still a poor loser.

Freddie was angry that Revolver was spreading rumors. "We never cheated, he did. He challenged us to a race, and when he was out of sight from the rest of the herd he was the one that would cut right in front of you. He would break your stride just so he could win."

Jeb's expression did not change. He had been at the racetrack long enough to know that everyone had a story to tell. Some were true and some were not, and stories did not matter when the starting gates opened.

"Well, all I know is what I heard. He's got those boys over there thinkin' you two are plannin' somethin' in today's race, so I thought I'd let you know what's goin' on, that's all."

He scratched again, and ambled off toward the hay barn. Freddie looked at Thunderball. "Did you hear that?"

Thunderball did not reply.

"What if all the others think we're going to cheat!"

"It doesn't matter," said Thunderball in his steady voice.

"It doesn't matter?" asked Freddie. He was surprised that Thunderball could take it so calmly.

"I mean it doesn't matter what Revolver says. We know it's not true, and for now all we can do is go out there and run the race. It's not important enough to get angry about."

Thunderball made sense. "You're right," said Freddie. "Revolver is just putting us down to make himself look good. I feel kind of sorry for him."

"So do I," Thunderball agreed. "But not sorry enough to slow down in the race."

"That's for sure."

Fifteen minutes before post time Freddie entered the paddock. Since this was a prep for the Kentucky Derby, the paddock gardens were crowded with people and reporters hoping to get a glimpse of a future Derby winner.

Freddie had drawn the number one post position, so he was the first horse out of the barn. As he was led around he caught a glimpse of Revolver. Remembering Thunderball's advice he gave him a simple nod of the head. Revolver responded with an aloof stare.

The horses were led onto the track where they warmed up from a jog to a slow gallop. This race was longer than any of the others. Instead of starting at the far side of the track and turning once to come to the homestretch, this time the race started in front of the grandstand and made a complete circle of the track.

By the time they were loaded into the starting gate Revolver was the farthest thing from Freddie's mind. He focused his attention on the gate ready to open at any moment.

The race started in a frenzy and they were on the track at a full gallop. At the first turn Freddie settled into fifth place, right behind Thunderball, and Revolver had taken a solid lead.

Down the backstretch, Freddie easily kept pace with Thunderball and the horses in second and third place. Revolver stayed in first place and showed no signs of tiring. When they came to the far turn, the other leaders began to waver, allowing Freddie and Thunderball to pass. The stablemates stayed even until they caught up to Revolver.

Coming into the homestretch the three horses were neck-and-neck, each one trying to extend himself beyond the others for the lead.

Revolver was near the inside rail, Thunderball was in the middle, and Freddie was in a good position on the outside. He could hear the sound of his own pounding heart and the heavy breathing of Thunderball to his side. This race had gone surprisingly easy so far. He realized that he was not as tired as he thought he would be at this point and his stride was still long and smooth. He was able to stretch out and pull to the lead as the finish line drew near. Freddie had left Thunderball, Revolver, and the rest of the field as he stretched out to the wire.

What he heard next was the most horrible sound he could ever imagine. A horse behind him fell to the ground with a thud, throwing his jockey and causing the rest of the horses to swerve to keep from trampling them.

Freddie's jockey hit him with his whip, urging him toward the finish line and preventing him from looking back. He used his last burst of energy to extend to a commanding lead and win the race.

The field of horses was eased and brought back to the grandstand. As Freddie approached, he could see a horse lying on his side in the middle of the homestretch. The horse raised his head and struggled to rise to his feet, but his right leg could not hold his weight. He went down again with a painful groan.

"Thunderball!" Freddie cried out in a shriek that echoed throughout the grandstand. He went wild trying to get free of his jockey so that he could go to Thunderball, but it was no use. In a second his groom was on the track, fastening a stud chain to his halter. Freddie reared in a desperate attempt to get away, but they led him to the winner's circle, where even the quiet, comforting voices of his owners could not calm him. Flashbulbs popped, but Freddie's eyes were on Thunderball.

As he was taken off the track he looked back to see Thunderball lying where he had fallen, his nose lifted toward the sky and his ears back, moaning as they lifted him into the ambulance.

Back at the barn Freddie heard no news of Thunderball. The empty stall next to him only made him more upset each time he looked into it. Frantically, he paced his stall, calling out every few minutes so loudly that the stablehands began to yell at him to be calm. He listened carefully each time someone passed the barn, hoping that Thunderball would return, but his hopes were futile.

Through most of the afternoon Freddie was unable to rest or eat. All he could do was pace his stall waiting for some news of his friend. Finally, he saw Jeb. The familiar limp of the old dog was a welcome sight.

"Have you heard anything about Thunderball?" Freddie asked.

"Yep. They've got him over at the hospital next door. They said he broke his leg, but he's gonna be all right," the dog replied.

Freddie sighed in relief. He had expected the worst. He worried that Thunderball was too injured to recover, and that it was all Revolver's fault.

"Then he'll be back soon?" Freddie asked.

"Nope. He ain't never comin' back here. His racing days is finished. They're planning on putting him out to stud.

Thought I'd tell you so you could calm down and get some rest."

He looked at Freddie, and Freddie saw a kind, understanding look in his eyes, one that he kept hidden under his hard exterior.

"Maybe it won't make you feel any better, but in all the years I've been here I've seen horses come and go. Some of them you like, some you don't, but Thunderball, well, I'm gonna miss him too."

Jeb stood by Freddie for a few moments, then without a word, ambled back to the tack room.

Freddie's heart sank. Thunderball would never race again. All that they had worked for was over. He thought about their first race up a grassy hill and how far they had come since then. Now, Thunderball would miss the biggest race of all. Freddie would run in the Kentucky Derby alone.

The next few days were hard. Another horse had been put in Thunderball's stall. He was a year younger than Freddie, the same age as they were when they were first brought to the track. He was excited and full of questions. Having someone new in his friend's stall was difficult. Freddie missed Thunderball too much. His appetite was gone, and he did not want to work out.

The day after the race his trainer thought he was just tired, but when there was no change in his behavior on the third and fourth day, the vet was called.

"Can't find a thing wrong with him," the vet told the trainer. "He's as healthy as he can be. I don't know why he's acting this way unless, hey, wasn't that his stablemate that went down the other day?"

The trainer nodded.

"Well, maybe he's just lonely. Happens all the time. Horses form strong attachments to each other. You might try taking him next door for a visit. Maybe seeing his buddy will lift his spirits."

"At this point I'll try anything," the trainer replied. "The Derby is in two weeks, and if he goes on like this we'll have to take him out of the race."

Early the next morning Freddie's owners came to visit. He was always glad to see them, and since Thunderball was gone the sight of them was all the more welcome.

"Come on, big guy," his owner said as he put Freddie's halter on. "We're going to see Thunderball."

The hospital was next door in a cinder-block barn. Each stall door had a screen over it so that the horses could see out. They stopped at the last stall, and opened the door for Freddie to see in.

Freddie looked in and saw Thunderball. His leg was in a cast, but he was able to stand.

"Thunderball!" exclaimed Freddie. He thought he would never see his friend again.

Thunderball looked up and whinnied with glee. "Hey Freddie! How are you?"

"I think I should be asking you that."

"Feeling better than I did the last time I saw you. The leg hurts a little but they say it's going to be OK. They're going to send me to one of those lay-up centers, you know, where I'll swim to get the strength back in my leg. They say it'll heal all right, but my racing days are over."

"I know, Jeb told me," Freddie said sadly. Thunderball was

being brave, like he always had been, but Freddie knew the disappointment he felt. They had been friends too long for him to be fooled.

"It's all Revolver's fault, isn't it? He cut in front of you just like that day in the pasture. He said he'd get you back some-day," Freddie said angrily.

"Revolver bumped me, but I can't say if he did it on purpose or not. It happened so fast," Thunderball replied. "My mother hurt her same leg."

Thunderball looked away from Freddie, and Freddie knew it was because he had tears in his eyes.

"I won't feel sorry for myself though, and I don't want you to feel sorry for me either. Jeb told me you're not trying your hardest in the morning. Why not?"

Now Freddie felt ashamed of himself. Thunderball was the one injured and Freddie was the one who was acting like he was hurt.

"I don't know. Just haven't felt like it I guess," he stammered, looking away.

"The Derby's in two weeks. You're going to have to work your hardest to win. No one is going to give that title to you. It's the chance of a lifetime, so don't miss it." Freddie could hear his voice start to crack.

"I won't," Freddie said, as tears filled his eyes. "I'm going to win this race for you because you deserve it."

"Win it for yourself, because you deserve it," Thunderball replied.

"I'll win it for both of us." Freddie bowed his head close to Thunderball's. "Take care of yourself, buddy."

For a moment they were like weanlings again. They looked

at each other the way they had when they played in the pasture. Only this time it was to say goodbye.

"You're good enough to win that race, don't you forget that," Thunderball said as Freddie left his stall.

Just then, Freddie remembered something his mother had told him. Sometimes you have to leave friends behind, but even if they are far away, they can still be close to your heart. True friends are forever.

CHAPTER TWELVE-A

Derby Day

DERBY DAY IS A DAY like no other. The excitement of the crowd is electric, as each person lifts his mint julep to toast the procession of horses. As tradition would have it, before the race a refrain of "My Ole Kentucky Home" echoes through the stands with nothing less than reverence.

For the participants, the excitement, tension, and anticipation envelop the surroundings. Cameras flash everywhere and reporters hound the trainers about the latest results of morning workouts.

Churchill Downs is in the heart of Louisville, Kentucky. The white clubhouse adorned with twin spires was richer in tradition than any racetrack Freddie had seen. This was special and he knew it. It was the chance he had dreamt of those long lonely nights when he was first separated from Romantic Myth. It was the goal he had strived to reach with every fatigued stride he took toward the finish line. It was the dream that gave him the desire to stay in front. This was a race that made champions, and it was all run for the blanket of roses awaiting the one horse fast enough to enter the winner's circle.

Accompanied by his owners and trainer, Freddie had arrived the week before the race. They took extra care to make him comfortable. Freddie's owners, who were normally unaffected by the prerace jitters, seemed more excited than usual, and they sensed the loneliness he felt for Thunderball.

Freddie thought of him often. What happened to Thunderball seemed so unfair. Of all the horses Freddie had known he had never met one with such dignity. His stablemate showed courage. Thunderball deserved to be in this race.

Perhaps it was that feeling that made Freddie want to win more than he had wanted anything in his entire life. He wanted it because it was the race they had pretended to run when they challenged each other as weanlings. They inspired each other then to do their very best. Now, in his heart, Thunderball was still there to encourage Freddie. He wanted to fill the emptiness that Thunderball must be feeling now that his life's dream was unattainable. Freddie hoped that somehow his friend could share in this victory if Freddie could only finish first. He knew he would have to beat Revolver and the best horses in the country to do it.

He also wanted to win for Romantic Myth. He wished that by the end of this day she could proudly say that her son had indeed remembered all that she had so lovingly taught him, that he had kept the last promise he made to her, to become the best he could be.

These thoughts comforted him and fueled his desire. Thunderball and Romantic Myth would love him still, whether he won or lost, and so would his owners and trainer. All they had ever encouraged him to do was his absolute best. Sharing this race with those who meant the most to him made it all the more important.

The race would begin soon, Freddie could sense it. The public address system announced that all horses running in the Derby were to be brought to the saddling area. He was taken from his stall and led toward the paddock. In the distance he could hear the national anthem echoing off the grandstand as it was played for thousands of fans who stood respectfully watching the red, white, and blue flag wave in the wind.

As he walked along, Freddie took notice of everything he passed. He did not want one detail of the day to go unremembered.

He saw the masses of people milling around the paddock area. The ladies were adorned in hats, and the men sported their finest suits. The horse in front of him looked very familiar. He had never raced against him before, but there was something about him that made him think they had met.

"What is your name?" Freddie called to him.

The colt turned. He had a finely chiseled face, and was very handsome.

"Rich Minute," the horse replied.

Instantly Freddie remembered where they had met. He was the colt in the next stall so very long ago when Romantic Myth had been at the hospital. He was the horse who first told Freddie about the Kentucky Derby, and now they were to race against each other for its title.

"I remember you," Freddie answered. "We met a very long time ago."

"I remember you too! You didn't know what this race was, and I had to explain it to you."

"That's right."

"Do you know now?" Rich Minute asked.

"Yes, only too well. Good luck today."

"Good luck to both of us," he said and turned his attention to the paddock.

Freddie saw his owners up ahead. They watched proudly as he was escorted to the saddling stall. His trainer put the saddle on his back and the bit in his mouth. His owners looked at him with more hope in their eyes than the very first time they watched him run in the pasture.

Freddie wanted them to know that he would not let them down, but all he could do was listen attentively to the words of encouragement they had to offer.

"Go to your horses, riders," the steward announced. "Riders up!" Freddie felt the familiar weight of his jockey as he mounted. It was time to go.

A trumpet sounded the famous call to the track as the post parade began. The crowd held their glasses high in the air and toasted the entrants with song. It was their way of recognizing the bravery it took for each horse and rider to make it this far.

Freddie pricked his ears up and pranced next to a calm lead horse as they made their way past the grandstand toward the starting gate. Revolver was two horses behind him. Twenty horses would run today, but Revolver was most on Freddie's mind.

"Don't just think about Revolver—you have to beat all the others too," Freddie admonished himself.

Finally they reached the start. The air was thick with anticipation, and the cheers of the crowd seemed muffled.

The race would start at the far end of the grandstand, passing it once and completing a full lap before passing it again.

One by one the horses were loaded into the gate. All of the work came down to this moment. The race would last only a few minutes, but the memories would last forever. Each knew there would be only one chance.

The bell sounded and the gates flew open.

They were on the track in a cloud of dust. Freddie was unable to see in front of him. He held his ground in the middle of the pack as they thundered down the homestretch for the first time. There were so many horses in the race and they were so tightly packed together that Freddie could only trust that his jockey could get out of the sea of runners. They were still in a close pack as they came into the first turn.

The horses bumped each other precariously as they funneled through the turn. A stumble by a front runner could have frightening consequences. If Freddie was going to win he would have to break away from them before he was unable to move at all. He waited patiently for the command from his jockey. "Don't be rattled," he thought to himself. "Don't be hurried. He'll tell me when to go." He tried to pace himself but knew he had to run now.

Revolver and Rich Minute were at the lead. Fighting his way to the front of the pack, Freddie was clinging to an uncertain third place.

Down the backstretch the riders held their horses in position. The thunder behind him was closing fast. Steadily,

Freddie sliced the sunlight between him and Revolver. The entire field was closing in again. As Freddie caught up to Revolver his front hooves clipped Revolver's back legs, breaking his stride. Freddie almost went down and his jockey lunged forward. The rider immediately pulled Freddie's head up so that he could recover his balance.

As they rounded the final turn the wall of sound was deafening. The crowd was on their feet. Freddie felt his jockey move him to the outside of the track. He was doing it. He caught up to Revolver. Rich Minute was tiring but able to stay with the two at the rail.

A tap from a left-handed whip was all the encouragement Freddie needed. Stubbornly, he ran with reckless abandon and passed the two, opening up a two-length lead at the top of the stretch. He ran all out, but he was beginning to tire. His jockey tried to slow him down, worried that he had made his final surge too soon and would not have enough energy left to finish.

Freddie began to falter. Revolver forgot his aching muscles and took aim at the chestnut colt.

He caught Freddie and matched his pace stride for stride with a quarter-mile to go. The two were breathing heavily and continuing to run when most of the others had long since given up. Rich Minute was a stride back, but the race was down to two.

Revolver moved past Freddie by a full length and Freddie could hear Rich Minute closing as he wavered and slowed. The finish line was too close to catch Revolver, and Rich Minute was now at Freddie's side.

Suddenly, his mind flashed to the pasture where he grew

up. It was him against Revolver, racing up the hill. Thunderball was there too, watching from beneath the oak tree.

Freddie dug in and ran faster. He ran on heart alone. He pulled away from Rich Minute and closed the gap on Revolver. As they came to the wire the two were dangerously close. Just yards before the finish line Freddie put his ears back and stretched his neck out.

"Remember to keep your head up and stretch it out as far as you can when you run. That will keep you in front when a race comes down to the wire," Royal Exile's words echoed through Freddie's mind.

He fixed his sights on the finish and gave it one last exhaustive effort. With all his strength he inched ahead of Revolver and crossed the finish line first.

He had won.

The crowd was still on their feet as he trotted back to the clubhouse on his way to the winner's circle. The exhilaration surpassed his grandest expectation. Freddie understood then what it was to be a champion, to prevail because he truly was the best horse to walk onto the track that day.

The blanket of red roses was placed across his withers. It was the sweetest aroma he had ever smelled.

As the photographers flashed pictures and well-wishers crowded closer for a look at the winner, Freddie's eyes met Revolver's. They looked at each other for a long moment, then Freddie nodded his head, affirming that Revolver was a rival deserving of his respect. His effort was valiant and fair. Revolver's eyes never wavered as he nodded back, conceding Freddie's victory.

Epilogue

ALTHOUGH FREDDIE WENT on to have other victories in his racing career, none was ever as sweet as that first Saturday in May when he became the champion of the Kentucky Derby. He did indeed go on to become a great racehorse and carry on the legend of his sire, Royal Exile.

When his racing days ended it was decided that Freddie would return to the farm where he was born. There he would stand next to his father and look out on the pasture where he grew up.

As the truck pulled down the drive to the farm Freddie thought that nothing had changed very much. He saw Patches sitting on the fencepost nearest the road. It made him happy to see her waiting.

When he stepped out of the trailer he could smell the freshly watered grass. The oak tree was still a commanding figure in the center of the yearling pasture, yet somehow did not look as tall as he remembered.

Immediately, Patches was at his feet, rubbing affection- ately against his legs.

"We heard that you were coming home, Freddie. I've spent every morning for the last week sitting on the fence looking up the road, waiting for you to come back," she purred.

Freddie bowed his neck and nuzzled her gently. "Thank you for waiting. I knew you'd be the first to meet me."

He was home, and as he walked past the pastures where he had once played he saw Thunderball in the distance. He looked like royalty with his prominent stature. His leg had healed just like the doctor had said.

"Freddie!" Thunderball called. "It's good to see you, my friend."

A tear came to Freddie's eye. It was like Romantic Myth had said, time and distance had not diminished their friend- ship.

"It's good to be home," Freddie replied.

In the distance Freddie could see a mare approaching his paddock. She walked slowly, but still her movement was graceful. She had a colt at her side. He was chestnut in color, but had a white star in the middle of his forehead. His long spindly legs made it apparent that he was not more than a few days old. He moved closer to her as she came near. She stopped a few feet away and took a long admiring look.

She looked into his eyes, and Freddie could see that her expression was full of love and pride as she looked upon him.

He struggled to say something. There was so much he wanted to share. He wanted to tell her about all the things he had seen and done since the last time they were together, but most of all he just wanted to tell her he loved her, and thank her for everything she had so lovingly taught him.

"Mother, I tried my best. I tried to remember all the things you taught me," was all that he could say.

She smiled and tears of happiness filled her eyes.

"Yes, Freddie," Romantic Myth replied, "you did."